Richard Gowing

Richard Cobden

Richard Gowing

Richard Cobden

ISBN/EAN: 9783337732059

Printed in Europe, USA, Canada, Australia, Japan

Cover: Foto ©ninafisch / pixelio.de

More available books at **www.hansebooks.com**

THE WORLD'S WORKERS.

Richard Cobden.

BY

RICHARD GOWING.

CASSELL & COMPANY, LIMITED:

LONDON, PARIS, NEW YORK & MELBOURNE.

[ALL RIGHTS RESERVED.]

1885.

CONTENTS.

RICHARD COBDEN.

CHAPTER I.

THE RESTLESSNESS OF GENIUS.

"WHAT is all this yearning after?" wrote Richard Cobden one day in a letter to his brother. "I can scarcely give myself a satisfactory answer. Surely not for money; I feel a disregard for it;" and in another part of the same confidential epistle, dwelling upon this state of his mind, he said: "Sometimes, I confess, I allow this sort of feeling to gain a powerful and harassing ascendancy over me. It disquiets me in the night as well as day."

Cobden was not, at the time when these restless, aching aspirations haunted him, an ambitious, dreaming boy, unacquainted with the practical and commonplace business of life. He was eight-and-twenty years of age. He had worked hard from his childhood. All the surroundings of his young career had been unromantic. No chance had ever been open to him of turning his remarkable energy of character to any other account than that of getting a living and helping to find the means of living for his father and his brothers and sisters. He had begun now to be a successful calico printer.

So far as we know of him it was only at this stage of mature manhood, when he had begun to see the substantial rewards of some fifteen years of close devotion to business, that the feeling grew upon him of a greater work for him to perform than he could find in the print works, or the counting-house, or the making of a fortune. It was "surely not for money." It was not for personal distinction. He became presently one of the most famous men of the century, but the work that he did was not done for his own profit or his own glory.

There is something curiously interesting in the almost sudden tokens, at this period of Cobden's life, of a high capacity for public affairs, and a clear mastery of some of the most difficult questions which engage the attention of rulers, statesmen, politicians, and social philosophers.

"What surprises one in reading the letters which Cobden wrote between 1833 and 1836," says Mr. John Morley,* "is the quickness with which his character widened and ripened. We pass at a single step from the natural and wholesome egotism of the young man who has his bread to win, to the wide interests and generous public spirit of the good citizen."

* "The Life of Richard Cobden," by John Morley (Chapman and Hall).

The wide interests and generous public spirit of the merely good citizen are suggested rather by the letters of the beginning than by those of the end of that three years. In 1835 he had written the famous pamphlet "England, Ireland, and America," a work which in a moment placed him in advance of the ablest and most experienced practical politicians of his day.

It does not take long to tell what Cobden's life had been up to the time of this restless and vague yearning to be doing something great and good in in the world.

CHAPTER II.

THE ANTECEDENTS OF GREATNESS.

RICHARD COBDEN is found, between five and ten years of age, attending a dame's school in the old rustic town of Midhurst, in Sussex, and, between school hours, looking after the sheep on his father's little farm called Guillard's Oak, near by. There were eleven children in the family, and he was the fourth. His father, a most kind, affectionate man, beloved by all his children, was unfortunate in his farming, and deficient in energy, and in 1813 his affairs went to ruin. Then the farm was sold. This was in 1814, when Richard Cobden (born in the neighbouring hamlet of Heyshott on the 3rd of June, 1804) was only ten years of age, and this was, unhappily for him, the end of his home life. The family was cast upon the bounty of his mother's relatives, one of whom sent him to school in Yorkshire, where, like poor Smike in a school, apparently very much of the character described in Dickens's novel, he was, Mr. Morley tells us, "from his tenth to his fifteenth year, ill-fed, ill-taught, ill-used;" never seeing parent or friend during the whole five years. It was, says Mr. Morley, a "cruel and disgusting mockery of an education;" but this, and his dame school work at Midhurst as a little child, was the sum total of his education and preparation for the life that lay before him.

Then the uncle who had paid for that unhappy schooling in Yorkshire took the poor boy into his counting-house at Old Change in the City of London as a junior clerk, and into his own house to live. Here is Mr. Morley's account of this not very cheerful stage in the young fellow's career :—

"Cobden's uncle and aunt expected servility in the place of gratitude, and, in his own phrase, 'inflicted rather than bestowed their bounties.' They especially disapproved of his learning French lessons in the early hours of the morning in his bedroom, and his fondness for book-knowledge was thought of evil omen for his future as a man of business. The position became so unpleasant that in 1822 Cobden accepted the offer of a situation in

a house of business at Ghent. It promised considerable advantages, but his father would not give his
approval, and Cobden, after some demur, fell in with
his father's wish. He remained where he was, and
did not quarrel. with such opportunity as he had
simply because he had missed a better."

So he was five years at the clerkship, and much of
his salary went towards the maintenance of his father's
household, at Westmean, near Alton, in Hampshire.
It was during this period that his mother died—his
mother to whom all the family were greatly devoted,
and from whom Richard Cobden seems to have
inherited some of the elements which by and by
ripened into the finest qualities in his character.

By 1825, when he was twenty-one years of age, he
had won good credit in the office at Old Change,
and was promoted to the position of a commercial
traveller. "Cobden's new position," says Mr. Morley
(whose most admirable biography is the sole authority
extant for the facts of Cobden's early life), "was
peculiarly suited to the turn of his character. Col-
lecting accounts and soliciting orders for muslins and
calicoes gave room in their humble sphere for those
high and inborn qualities of energy and sociability
which in later years produced the most active and
the most persuasive of popular statesmen. But what
made the life of a traveller so specially welcome to
Cobden was the gratification that it offered to the
master-passion of his life: *an insatiable desire to know*

the affairs of the world. Famous men who became his friends in the years to come agree in the admission, that they have never known a man in whom this trait of a sound and rational desire to know and to learn was so strong and so inexhaustible."

He saw much of England, Ireland, and Scotland in the four years during which he was engaged as a commercial traveller. Then he entered into partnership with two young men, and the three began business on their own account, with a very small capital, more than half of which was borrowed. It was still the business of commercial travelling, but the commercial travellers were their own masters, taking orders for muslins and calicoes on their own responsibility on commission, and passing the orders on to the manufacturers with whom they had made arrangements. This involved being well trusted by manufacturers. On this enterprise they went to Manchester, and this is a passage from a letter of Cobden's on the incident: "We introduced ourselves to Fort Brothers & Co., a rich house, and we told our tale honestly, concealing nothing. In less than two years, from 1830, we owed them forty thousand pounds for goods which they had sent to us in Watling Street, upon no other security than our characters and knowledge of our business. I frequently talked with them in later times upon the great confidence they showed in men who avowed that they were not possessed of £200 each. Their answer was that they would always prefer to trust young men with connections, and with a knowledge of their trade, if they knew them to possess character and ability, to those who started with capital without these advantages, and that they had acted on this principle successfully in all parts of the world."

Success in this enterprise led Mr. Cobden and his partners to make the experiment of printing their own calicoes. They opened works at Sabden, in Lancashire, and presently they were carrying on business in a large way in Manchester and in London, Richard Cobden having introduced his elder brother Frederick into the Manchester branch of the business. This brings us to 1832, when Cobden was twenty-eight years of age.

CHAPTER III.

HIS EDUCATION.

IT takes a high degree of education to play the part that Richard Cobden played in the world for the thirty-five years or so after he had become a success-ful Lancashire calico printer. What was Cobden's education? And how did he come by it?

His time was, to all appearance, fully occupied with practical affairs from the day when he left the miserable Yorkshire school at fifteen years of age and entered the counting house at Old Change until the day of his death, nearly half a century later. There never was an interval set apart for study. There is no account of his having ever sought formal instruction or scholastic aid. Yet he was not only a man of immense information on a very wide range of subjects; but he was, in all but the technical or pedantic sense, a scholar. He is not to be classed with the men of great natural ability who have played important parts on the stage of life without learning. He could take his place as an equal in any society; and among men of education and culture he was in a broad and general sense a man of culture, education, and refinement.

At the Yorkshire school in his childhood he earned trifles of pocket-money by writing letters for his little school-fellows to their parents. As a boy at Old Change, he kept a little diary of his petty expenses which is still in the possession of his friends, and among the items are trifles for the purchase of "Brougham on Popular Education," "Franklin's Essays," and "Childe Harold." By way of exercise he kept this little record in crude French, of which the following examples are quoted by Mr. Morley: "*charité*, 1s.; *donné un pauvre garçon*, 1d.; *un pauvre garçon*, 2d.." Of Cobden at the age of twenty-eight, close upon that turning point in his life when the claims of business and of private affairs had begun to be too little for the range and aspirations of his mind, we find Mr. Morley reporting of him: "Even at a moment when he might readily have been excused for thinking only of money and muslins, he felt and obeyed the necessity for knowledge, but for knowledge as an instrument, not as a luxury. When he was immersed in the first pressing anxieties of his new business at Manchester he wrote to his brother in London: 'Might we not in the winter instruct ourselves a little in mathematics? I have a great disposition, too, to know a little Latin, and six months would suffice if I had a few books. Can you trust to your perseverance to stick to them? I think I can. I wish Henry [another brother] to take lessons in Spanish this winter; it is most useful as a commercial language.'"

It was only three years after this that Cobden wrote his famous essay on "England, Ireland, and America," and these are some of Mr. Morley's remarks on the evidence in this work of his wide and varied reading: "This pamphlet, and that which followed in the next year ["Russia"], show by their references and illustrations that the writer, after his settlement in Manchester in the autumn of 1832 [the time when he planned the study of mathematics and Latin], had made himself acquainted with the greatness of Cervantes, the geniality of Le Sage, the sweetness of Spenser, the splendid majesty of Burke, no less than with the general course of European history in the past, and the wide forces that were then actually at work in the present."

It might have been added that these essays prove Cobden to have had, at that time, the principles of Adam Smith, and of the successors of that great master of political economy, as clearly in his mind for application at any moment as the figures of the multiplication table.

His knowledge in the wide field of history, politics, and international commerce was almost unequalled. Professor Thorold Rogers says : " If exact and careful knowledge of history constitutes learning, Cobden was, during the years of his political career, the most learned speaker in the House of Commons. Dealing as he did with broad questions of public policy, he got up his case accurately and laboriously. His facts, culled from all sources, were judiciously selected and were never challenged. A cautious student of political economy, he knew that this science, the difficulty of which he fully recognised, was or ought to be eminently inductive, and that an economist without facts is like an engineer without materials or tools."

At a later period all the world took it as a matter of course that Cobden should negotiate the commercial treaty with the Emperor Napoleon III. and his Ministers, and this he did with all the ease of an accomplished diplomatist to whom the French language is one of the principal equipments of his profession, writing and publishing in French, making speeches in French, and sitting in council with Frenchmen to deal in the language of the country with the minutest and most cross-grained technicalities of manufacture, commerce, and tariffs. He travelled all over Europe, holding intercourse with sovereigns, statesmen, distinguished men of all orders and degrees, merchants, manufacturers, and others, with only the occasional and exceptional assistance of an interpreter. "Everywhere," says Mr. Morley, "men were delighted by his tact and address. He made as captivating points in a speech to the traders of Cadiz, the farmers of Perugia, or the great nobles in Rome, as when, from a waggon, he had addressed the rustics of a village in the West of England. At Milan he charmed them by mentioning that if they went into a London merchant's office they would find the accounts kept on a method which came from Italy; and that the great centre of our financial system was in a street that was still named from the Lombard bankers. At Florence he warmed the hearts of those who listened to him by saying that he had come to Tuscany with the feelings of a believer visiting the shrines of his faith; the Dutch and the Swiss owed to their geographical situation a partial escape from the Protective system, but to Tuscany belonged the glory of preceding the rest of the world by half a century in applying economic theories to legislation." "Let us render solemn homage," cried Richard Cobden in this historic speech, "to the memory of the great men who gave the world a lesson so memorable in the science of government; honour to Bandini, who a century ago perceived the truth that Free Trade is the only sure instrument of prosperity; immortal honour to Leopold, who, seizing the lamp of science from the hands of Bandini, entered boldly into the ways of Free Trade, then obscure and unknown, without flinching before the obstacles that ignorance, prejudice, and selfishness had strewn in the path; honour to Neri, to Fabroni, to Fossombroni—to all those statesmen, in a word, who have preserved down to our own days the great work of their master, Bandini."

These extracts and memoranda carry us a long way into those days when Cobden was in the midst of the great work for which he was vaguely yearning at eight-and-twenty, and a long way beyond the time of his laying out the Manchester winter evenings for the study of mathematics and Latin with his brother Frederick. But it goes to show that with an exceedingly unfavourable start, and without any visible time or opportunity for great feats of self-education and self-culture, he became by and by, to all practical intents and purposes, one of the best informed and most accomplished men in Europe.

And then, apart from his reading, his culture, his great information, there was his remarkable excellence as a writer. Those first pamphlets of his on "England, Ireland, and America," and on "Russia," written, the one only three, and the other four years after the time of the commencement of his business operations in Manchester, were, putting aside for the moment the important subjects and the masterly treatment, quite great feats of English literature. Here is the opinion of Mr. Morley, a most competent judge, on this point. Speaking of "the literary excellence of these performances," he says :

"They have a ringing clearness, a genial vivacity, a free and confident mastery of expression which can hardly be surpassed. . . . What is striking in Cobden is, that after a lost and wasted childhood, a youth of drudgery in a warehouse, and an early manhood passed amid the rather vulgar associations of the commercial traveller, he should, at the age of one-and-thirty, have stepped forth the master of a written style which, in boldness, freedom, correctness, and persuasive moderation, was not surpassed by any man then living."

Cobden's was a name unknown when his first pamphlet was published, and this essay and the one which followed it in the next year on "Russia," were announced as written by "A Manchester manufacturer." They had a very large circulation, and as an example of the impression which they made on the minds of many readers accustomed to the discussion of great questions of politics, Mr. F. W. Chesson relates the following anecdote with respect to the essay on "Russia." "Shortly after the publication of the pamphlet, Lord Durham, who

B

was then the English Ambassador at St. Petersburg, received a copy of it in his official bag. He read it, and was so much impressed with the clearness and force of its leading ideas that he at once wrote to his friend, the late lamented Mr. Joseph Parker, and requested him to discover the name of the author. Mr. Parker obtained Mr. Cobden's permission to mention his name; and when, two years later, his lordship returned to England, he desired Mr. Parker to bring about a meeting between himself and Mr. Cobden. The result was that Mr. Cobden dined with Lord Durham, who, after an evening of friendly conversation, was still more struck with his new acquaintance. His subsequent prophetic and sagacious remark to Mr. Parker deserves to be recorded: 'Mark my words,' he said, 'Cobden will one day be one of the first men in England.'"

The earlier essay Mr. John Bright has spoken of as "a pamphlet, I venture to say, of such sagacity and foresight that it has probably never been excelled by any essay on politics in modern times."

"Cobden always felt that much of what is best worth knowing is never written in books," says Mr. Morley. He studied affairs at home and abroad, face to face with the facts. He was a splendid observer, and a wonderfully keen and sound reasoner upon the things that he saw. He visited France in 1833; France and Switzerland in 1834; and America in 1835. Then he wrote his pamphlet on "Russia;" and in 1836 he made a six months' journey to the East, visiting Lisbon, Cadiz, Malta, Cairo, Alexandria, Constantinople, Smyrna and Athens. By this time he had learned much indeed of what the world had to teach to such a man. His letters abound with the most interesting and suggestive comment. "He had laid up," says Mr. Morley, "a great stock of political information, and acquired a certain living familiarity with the circumstances of the Eastern basin of the Mediterranean and the Turkish Government, then, as now, the centre of our active diplomacy, and with the real working of those principles of national policy which he had already condemned by the light of common sense and reflection."

Such was his preparation for the public career upon which he was now about to enter.

CHAPTER IV.

THE POLITICS OF COMMERCE.

" A BAGMAN'S millennium " is the description of the aim and purpose of Mr. Cobden's policy given by a lady in a fashionable drawing-room, some six years after the repeal of the Corn Laws, in the presence of Cobden's friend, Mr. George Combe. Cobden the commercial traveller was the "bagman," and the " millennium " was the golden time when, without any

let or hindrance, everybody should be free to " buy in
the cheapest market and sell in the dearest."

It was a clever and scoffing way of depreciating
Cobden's political faith ; but there is something in
the epigram which may help the student to grasp
the great Free Trader's doctrine. Put in a broad,
rough way, it is the doctrine that the prosperity and
happiness of mankind depend chiefly upon the
cultivation and maintenance of the conditions most
favourable to the pursuits of industry and trade. In
the struggle for existence there should be the same
chance for all ; and nations, like individuals, should
take measures to " make ends meet."

Politicians and statesmen had not been in the
habit of looking into the science of legislation and
government from that point of view when Mr. Cobden
began seriously to consider public affairs. It was a
point of view to be found in the books of the political
economists, but Cobden was in some degree the first—
and certainly in his day, and in any day thus far, the
ablest, and the clearest-headed—of those who had
applied the doctrine to the actual, practical politics of
the time. He put much of his opinion of the changes
which ought to be made in our system of managing
the country's affairs into his first pamphlet, " England,
Ireland and America," and he began with what has
been called the " Balance of power."

It was the opinion of pretty nearly all the statesmen of Europe that it was necessary to preserve,

among the European countries, such a balance in point of power that no one or two or three should be strong enough to do what they pleased in spite of the rest. Thus, when Napoleon Bonaparte was not only Emperor of the French but master of Italy, Spain, Belgium and Holland, Europe was out of "balance," and all the countries were in danger.

Now Cobden regarded the notion of the "balance of power" as, to a very large extent, a mischievous superstition. He never went so far as to say that, when there was good reason to believe that the safety of this country was threatened, the Government should not proceed to protect itself or to attack the enemy ; but he was of the opinion that England had always been a great deal too ready to set all the world to rights ; that in almost every case of our interference, for ages past, the wars we entered upon were not necessary for our safety or welfare ; that our inter- ference did little or no real or permanent good ; and that, besides the awful bloodshed and the horrors, these wars inflicted immeasurable cost, debt and misery upon our people at home, and were a vast hindrance to the work of civilisation amongst us.

The very first paragraph of his first essay was upon this subject, and here are two or three of the sentences : " History exhibits us, at different periods, in the act of casting our sword into the scale of every European state. In the meantime events have pro- claimed, but in vain, how futile must be our attempts to usurp the sceptre of the Fates. Empires have arisen unbidden by us; others have departed despite our utmost efforts to preserve them. All have undergone a change so complete that, were the writers who only a century ago lauded the then existing state of the balance of Europe to reappear, they would be startled to find, in the present relations of the continent, no vestige of that perfect adjustment which had been purchased at the price of so much blood."

This first essay was written at a time when there was reason to fear that we might go to war with Russia in defence of the Turkish Empire, and Mr. Urquhart, a distinguished politician and diplomatist, had written a pamphlet to prove that it would be the duty and the right policy of England to fight on the side of Turkey against the aggression of Russia. Mr. Urquhart's appeal met with much favour among politicians, and in combating it Mr. Cobden set forth his own principles very clearly. It is not necessary for us to follow him into the reasons why, in his opinion, Turkey did not deserve protection at our hands. He laid it down as an axiom to start with: "That no government has the right to plunge its people into hostilities except in defence of their own national honour or interests. Unless this principle be made the rule of all, there can be no guarantee for the peace of any one country so long as there may be found a people whose grievances may attract the sympathy or invite the interference of another state."

In that passage will be found a limitation as well as a statement of Cobden's doctrine of "non-intervention," which has been so much discussed. He did not say that a country should not fight for its honour or interests; and when in after years he opposed himself so strenuously to our wars and our preparations for wars he did not depart from this qualification of the principle of non-intervention; he simply argued in each case that neither honour nor interest nor policy warranted the hostile action of this country in the particular quarrel then under discussion.

Proceeding in this essay to combat Mr. Urquhart's views, he says: "Great Britain has, in contempt of the dictates of prudence and self-interest, an insatiable thirst to become the peacemaker abroad; or, if that benevolent task fail her, to assume the office of gendarme and keep in order, gratuitously, all the refractory nations of Europe. Hence does it arise that, with an invulnerable island for our territory, more secure against foreign molestation than is any part of the coast of North America, we magnanimously disdain to avail ourselves of the privileges which Nature offers to us, but cross the ocean in quest of quadripartite treaties or quadruple alliances, and, probably, to leave our own good name in pledge for the debts of the poorer members of such confederacies. To the same spirit of over-weening national importance may in great part be traced the ruinous wars and yet more ruinous subsidies of our past history."

These are the foremost points of the principle of non-intervention insisted upon in this first essay. The application of his case to the immediate question at issue—the merits of the then suggested interference between Russia and Turkey—is voluminous. It is in the course of this argument that Mr. Cobden had no hesitation in avowing his deliberate conviction that "not merely Great Britain, but the entire civilised world, will have reason to congratulate itself the moment when that territory [Turkey] again falls beneath the sceptre of any other European power whatever." And he added: "Ages must elapse before that favoured region will become, as it is by Nature destined to become, the seat and centre of commerce, civilisation, and true religion; but the first step towards this consummation must be to convert Constantinople again into that which every lover of humanity and peace longs to behold it—the capital of a Christian people."

Then he comes back to the principle which is the backbone of the essay on " England," that we must keep out of wars, for wars stop civilisation, prosperity, and liberty; and we must cultivate peace, industry, and *trade*. The last word is the keystone. "*Commerce* is the grand panacea which, like a beneficent medical discovery, will serve to inoculate with the healthy and saving taste for civilisation all the nations of the world. Not a bale of merchandise leaves our shores but it bears the seeds of intelligence and fruitful thought to the members of some less enlightened community ; not a merchant visits our seats of manufacturing industry but he returns to his own country the missionary of freedom, peace, and good government; whilst our steamboats that now visit every port of Europe, and our miraculous railroads that are the talk of all nations, are the advertisements and vouchers for the value of our enlightened institutions."

Nothing but trade can make or save the country. " The self-same impulse," says Cobden, " drew all nations at different periods of history to Tyre, to Venice, and to Amsterdam ; and if, in the revolution of time and events, a country should be found (which is probable) whose cottons and woollens shall be cheaper than those of England and the rest of the world, then to that spot—even should it, by supposition, be buried in the remotest nook of the globe— will all the traders of the earth flock ; and no human power, no fleets or armies, will prevent Manchester, Liverpool, and Leeds, from sharing the fate of their once proud predecessors in Holland, Italy, and Phœnicia."

So ran the political creed. The destinies of nations depend upon trade. Peace means trade, and trade makes peace. Non-intervention in the quarrels of other nations fosters trade. Whatever hinders trade must be banished. We must produce at the cheapest rate, and supply the markets of the world at the lowest price, and whatever stands in the way of these conditions of business is a thing to be looked into and got rid of if possible. The wars that interfered with business also gave us a National Debt. The National Debt is a constant expense which hinders us from producing goods as cheaply as otherwise we might produce them. The National Debt should therefore be reduced as quickly as possible by present self-denial and sacrifice, and we must keep out of wars in order to keep down the debt.

And thus it is that Ireland and America come into the set of essays in this first pamphlet of Cobden's. Let us see how the argument runs.

Ireland was in a bad state. It was unprosperous, neglected, wretched, degraded. This is how Cobden led up to his description of the condition of that unhappy country : "Whilst within the last twenty years our sympathies have gone forth over the whole of Europe in quest of nations suffering from or rising up against the injustice of their rulers; whilst Italy, Greece, Spain, France, Portugal, Turkey, Belgium, and Poland, have successively filled the newspapers with tales of their domestic wrongs ; and whilst our diplomatists, fleets, and armies have been put in motion at enormous cost to carry our counsel, or, if needful, our arms, to the assistance of the people of those remote regions : it is an unquestionable fact that the population of a great portion of our own empire has, at the same time, presented a grosser spectacle of moral and physical debasement than is to be met with in the whole civilised world."

He goes on to describe the state of Ireland, points out the causes of the mischief, and suggests remedies; but the point of the whole story is, that while the remedies are not applied Ireland is "a diseased member of the body politic;" and hence, when we go forth into the world's markets with our products, we are like a lame man entering for a race. Other men had preached to the world of the wrongs and the woes of Ireland; it remained for Cobden to point out that, while we gained nothing and lost much by attempting to fight the battle of strangers against those who wronged or oppressed them, by leaving Ireland in this condition we were doing much to disqualify ourselves for competing with other countries in the productions of our labour and our manufacture.

The whole moral was enforced in the third essay by a consideration of the resources and prospects of America. The great Republic of the United States did not interfere in the quarrels of other countries; it had no wars, a merely nominal standing army, no Ireland hung round its neck, and not much National Debt. It bade fair to be our great rival in its products and its manufactures.

To maintain and improve our position as a nation, to be a wealthy, a prosperous, a well-conditioned and happy people, we must shake ourselves clear of everything that stands in the way of the success and

the extension of our manufacture and our commerce ;
and having passed in review our hindrances in the
shape of unnecessary, useless, and mischievous wars,
standing armies, extravagant defences, great public
debt, and some other stumbling blocks and burdens,
Cobden worked round to the Corn Laws, and these
appear to have been the first words he ever wrote on
this subject, at a time when he had as yet taken no
serious part in the long-standing agitation for free
trade in corn. He would, it may be taken for granted,
have been found ranged with the Free Traders so
soon as he was brought into any sort of relationship
with political controversy, by whatever direction he
might have reached the subject. But these essays are
clear demonstration at the very threshold of his public
career that the Repeal of the Corn Laws presented
itself to him as a necessary part of his broad theory
that, in the scheme of civilisation—in order to compass
the greatness of a country and the welfare and comfort of its whole population—a nation must be worked
very much as if it were a large trading concern, culti-
vating all the conditions favourable to business, re-
moving out of the way all obstacles to business, and
avoiding any line of conduct tending to interfere with
the success of business. Thus was Free Trade with
him a section of a large theory of politics, and the
more he applied his mind to the development of his
political view, the more he became convinced of the
exceptional and surpassing importance of Free Trade

as an element in the scheme : until by-and-by he saw in Free Trade itself the means by which all the other articles of his political faith might, in the long process of time, be realised.

In these first essays, however, the repeal of the Corn Laws is simply a means to the end of enabling the people to bear the national burdens and to enter, on so much the more favourable terms, into rivalry with other countries for the world's custom in the world's markets.

He proceeded to argue in this way : The Corn Laws as they stood were "founded on the principle of limiting, as far as possible, the growth of the population of Great Britain within the means of the soil to supply it with subsistence." " No candid advocate of a Protective duty," he said, " will . . . . dispute that to restrict the import of corn into a manufacturing nation is to strike out the life of its foreign commerce." Here is the arithmetic of the position : "The whole area of the cultivated land of this monarchy is estimated at about forty-five millions of acres ; at twenty pounds an acre the fee simple of the soil of these islands (we of course leave out the houses, &c.) would very little exceed the interest of our debt. There is an end, therefore, of the idea of discharging the principal out of the real property of the country ; and by what means would they who obstruct a foreign commerce profess to pay the interest of the debt without the assistance of that trade ? "

Mr. Cobden supposes himself to be speaking to people who have either a very clear insight into the operation of the laws of trade, or who are familiar with some of the simplest elements of political economy. He did not consider it necessary to explain that a people who had to pay from eighty to a hundred shillings a quarter for wheat could not possibly make goods cheaply enough to sell them in the markets of the world ; and he took it for granted that every man who gave consideration to public questions knew that if, by import duties, we kept foreign produce out of our markets, it was a law like a law of Nature that our productions could not be purchased by foreigners, since the foreigner would have no means of paying for our goods except by sending us his productions, which would be excluded by our duties. Hence he soon arrived at this clinching argument : "The question of the Repeal of the Corn Laws, then, resolves itself into one of absolute State necessity ; since our foreign trade, which is indispensable to the payment of the interest of the National Debt, cannot be permanently preserved if we persevere in a restrictive duty against the principal article of exchange of rude, unmanufacturing people. To prohibit the import of corn, such as is actually the case at this moment, is to strangle infant commerce in its cradle."

CHAPTER V.

SUPERSTITIONS OF TRADE.

FREE TRADE was, therefore, but one article—though a very important and essential one—in Cobden's political creed. It was no discovery of his, but he saw, perhaps more clearly than any other man before him, that it was a part of a scheme of statesmanship without which, as the competition of nations went on, no country would be able to hold its own. Soon after he had written those essays he had begun to be drawn into the great Free Trade agitation, which had been going on, and becoming keener and fiercer year by year, before his own attention had been turned to the consideration of these questions.

What, then, was this memorable agitation whereof by-and-by he became first the great leader, and then at length the victorious champion?

It is a long story, that fills many books. In all the annals of England there is not a more interesting chapter of history, nor one better illustrating the character of Englishmen and the struggles whereby the country has been made what it is.

Politics, like all other branches of study, have been beset by superstitions. Perhaps the most unfortunate and mischievous of commercial superstitions is that known as the theory of the "Balance of trade."

Somehow men got into their heads the curious notion that it is good for a country to sell its products to other countries but not so good to purchase commodities from abroad. It was admitted that it might be a benefit to take foreign products in exchange for our own ; but it was thought that we ought to be very careful not to buy more foreign goods than we sold of English goods, lest, by paying the balance in gold, we reduced our stock of money and so became poorer. This fallacy is hundreds and even thousands of years old. It has been forgotten— rather than exposed or refuted—at times, and it has at other times taken fresh and active possession of men's minds. Its actual scientific refutation is not much more than a hundred years old. Adam Smith, the father of the science of political economy, was the first to clearly demonstrate that the balance of trade theory is a fallacy and a delusion ; but the error is not dead yet. In every period of commercial depression people will be found looking round for the causes of the temporary adversity and reviving this old superstition. They will say, "The people are suffering because money is going out of the country in the purchase of foreign goods while it ought to be expended in the country upon articles of home produce."

Perhaps the mistake arises, in the first instance, from a fallacious comparison between the case of the nation and that of the individual. Because a person parts with his money in the purchase of goods, and is seen to become poorer as his cash diminishes, it is thought to be the same with the nation. But it is not so. Buying and selling between nations is not a matter of money at all; it is a pure matter of exchanging one sort of goods for another. The foreigner will not let us have his goods unless we give him at once the English goods that he wants, by way of payment. Our money would not be so useful to the foreign merchant as our goods, because he can sell our goods at home or elsewhere at a profit. Sometimes, by way of settling up accounts between English exporters and foreign exporters, a comparatively small amount of gold coin or solid gold passes from one country to another, but it very soon comes back again.

Why does it come back?

Because a certain amount of money is needed in this country, and a certain amount in any other country, for the convenient transaction of business. The value of all the gold and silver in England is roughly estimated to be equivalent to about £140,000,000. Now it is a law in currency and trade that when gold is cheap goods are dear, and when goods are cheap gold is dear. The law is as undoubtedly true as is the rule that twice two are four. This can be easily shown, thus: Suppose a sheep is worth three sovereigns on the first of May, and suppose a sheep of the same weight and quality were worth

c

four sovereigns on the first of June : then we should
say sheep are dearer in June than in May.   But that
would be the same thing as to say that, in the sheep
market, gold is *cheaper* in June than in May.   On
the first date one could get more sheep for his gold ;
on the second date more gold for his sheep.   This
must be very clear.   And there is another simple
but · absolutely certain law, that whatever useful
thing is scarce is dear, and whatever useful thing
is plentiful is cheap.   If sheep are plentiful they
will be cheap ; if they are scarce they will be dear.
The rule is as good for gold as for sheep.   If
sovereigns are plentiful they will be cheap (that is
to say, they will buy fewer sheep) ; if they are scarce
they will be dear (and will buy more sheep).   Therefore, if we send a few millions of sovereigns out of
the country to pay a balance between English and
foreign merchants, sovereigns will become to that
extent more scarce in England, and therefore dearer,
and all English goods in the market will be so much
the cheaper ; while in the country to which those
millions of sovereigns went (say France), there will be
for the moment an excess of gold, and in France
gold will be cheap and goods dear.   What follows?
Why, the French merchant immediately finds out
the state of things.   He hears that English goods
are unusually cheap, while French goods are unusually dear.   He buys a cargo of English goods
for the French market for the sake of the profit ; and

as gold is just then plentiful in France and scarce in England, he pays gold into England for his cargo of English goods. So we quickly get back our usual quantity of gold. In fact, in the natural process of trade between nation and nation, gold finds its level, just as water will find its level. And this is very much the same thing as saying that, except in a temporary and comparatively trifling way, in the trade between one country and another, goods are paid for by goods and not by money.

But the important part of this truth is that it puts an end to the fallacy about the "balance of trade." It shows that we need never be afraid of buying too many goods from other countries, because we may be quite satisfied that the other countries will take our goods (and not our money) in exchange. That is what it comes to, very quickly, in spite of any little temporary disturbance of the rule in the operations of commerce.

That being so, clearly the best thing that any country can do is to sell to other nations what can be produced most cheaply at home, and to buy of those peoples what they can produce more cheaply than we. It is the secret of getting the largest possible results for our labour. Adam Smith, the discoverer of the scientific theory of Free Trade, illustrated the case in a very lucid passage of his famous book, the "Wealth of Nations," in a comparison between the case of the nation and that of the

individual, which is sound, and free in every respect
from the slightest suggestion of fallacy. This is the
passage: "It is the maxim of every prudent master of
a family never to attempt to make at home what it
will cost him more to make than to buy. The tailor
does not attempt to make his own shoes, but buys
them of the shoemaker. The shoemaker does not
attempt to make his own clothes, but employs a tailor.
The farmer attempts to make neither the one nor the
other, but employs those different artificers. All of
them find it for their interest to employ their whole
industry in a way in which they have some advantage
over their neighbours, and to purchase with a part of
its produce, or what is the same thing, with the price
of a part of it, whatever else they have occasion for."

The very heart of the principle of Free Trade is
in those few sentences. It is of universal application.
Whoever thinks that he has discovered a case in
which the principle should not be applied has made a
mistake somewhere.

It is a mistake which has been made at one time
or another by every civilised nation, and it prevails
over nearly all the countries of the world at the
present moment. The method of limiting or preventing the importation of foreign goods is by a tax
on imports. At the time when Richard Cobden was
passing from the days of youth to those of manhood,
when he was watching and studying public affairs at
the same time that he was pursuing the avocation

first of a "bagman," and then of a merchant and calico printer, almost a Chinese wall of taxation upon imports was built up around our shores. "In 1824," says Mr. A. Mongredien,* "there was hardly an article obtainable from abroad that was admissible here without the payment of import duties, always heavy, sometimes excessive, and in certain cases all but prohibitory. It mattered not whether it was a raw material or a manufactured product, whether it was an article of luxury or of universal consumption, whether it came in masses, like cotton, or in driblets, like orchilla—everything foreign which an Englishman might use was withheld from him till its cost had been enhanced by a customs' duty. The tariff list of the United Kingdom formed a tolerably complete dictionary of all the products of human industry."

The balance of trade theory, and the attempt of the legislature to "protect British industry" by reversing that maxim of every "prudent master of a family," which we have quoted from Adam Smith on page 36, had brought old England to the very edge of ruin, and its people to starvation and destitution, at the time when Richard Cobden began to feel that mysterious yearning to put his hand to some task which drew him presently into the midst of the great strife of public affairs. Adam Smith, the first thinker to demonstrate the truth about trade, has been called

* "History of the Free Trade Movement" (Cassell & Company)

the father of political economists; Richard Cobden, fifty years later, came to be described as the "Apostle of Free Trade."

CHAPTER VI.

THE CORN LAWS.

RICHARD COBDEN appeared upon the scene of public life and political agitation in the interval between two of the greatest measures in Parliament of this century : the Reform Bill of 1832, and the Repeal of the Corn Laws in 1846. He was the mere spectator of the first of those great achievements in our political progress; he was the hero of the second.

Of all the taxes on foreign goods, the most famous in the history of tariffs is the English duty on corn. It brought the country more than once within a very little of revolution. It drove the old English constitution to a dead-lock. Out of it grew the greatest and best-managed political agitation on record—that of the Anti-Corn-Law League. It made Free Trade a burning question all over the civilised world ; and, whenever the time shall come for free tariffs among the nations, the world will know that the people were ripe for the triumph of the doctrine of Adam Smith's "Wealth of Nations" the sooner by a generation or two because of the Corn Laws, and the League, and Richard Cobden.

Even though Cobden was deeply immersed in business matters in 1832, when the great Reform Bill was passed, and though his biography by Mr. Morley goes to show that the passion for public affairs had not then taken that overwhelming possession of his mind of which there was such strong evidence only two or three years later, it will always be to some extent a puzzling fact that, from the age of twenty-five to twenty-eight, while the country was nearly mad about the franchise and popular representation, he was almost silent, while only two or three years later his whole soul was aroused into action in the movement for the Repeal of the Corn Laws.

That is an interesting point for the consideration of the student of character among great men. The more closely the career of Cobden is analysed, the more clearly will it be seen that the bent of his mind was for practical legislation and the administration of public affairs, rather than for the making or mending of the constitution. He worked with the reformers of the constitution from the time of his entering upon political life until the day of his death, and he was a reformer among the reformers; but always the greater part of his energy and labour, and all the keenness of his interest, were not in such questions as the qualification of the voter, the ballot, or the area of Parliamentary representation, but in the freedom of commerce, free navigation, imperial finance, peace, our

foreign and colonial relations, local and municipal
government, and education. His gifts were the gifts of
practical statesmanship. Coming into the world at
that period in our history, and with his peculiar and
remarkable insight into the political needs of the time,
circumstances made him the greatest and most successful of political agitators. From that field of work
England could not afford to spare him. Nevertheless,
at a different time, and under a different set of circumstances, he would have done great things in the
highest walks of statesmanship. Indeed, though he
was never in office as a member of any Government,
and had no hand in the making of any statute, or in
any act of administration except the French Commercial Treaty, the influence of his life and the ideas
that he has left on record have had a very large influence on the statesmanship of the country, both in
legislation and administration, from the date of his
death until the present time.

Even Cobden, however, and the Anti-Corn-Law
League, would have found it impossible to get the
Corn Laws repealed but for the triumph of the Reform
Bill of 1832. It is necessary to remember this in
order to understand the story of the Anti-Corn-Law
agitation previous to the time when Cobden's ability,
energy, and singleness of purpose carried him to the
front. The Reform Act of 1832 made the repeal of
the Corn Laws possible ; but, on the other hand, it was
the misery in the land caused by the cruel pressure of

the Corn Laws which added to the reform agitation the irresistible force that gave the reformers the victory in 1832. In the seventeen years from the battle of Waterloo to the passing of the Reform Bill there was never a reform meeting, or a reform demonstration, at which the Corn Laws were not denounced. But everybody knew that there was no hope for the repeal of the Corn Laws by the unreformed Parliament.

During many hundreds of years before Cobden's time the Government of England had attempted, by numerous enactments, to regulate the supply of corn. Sometimes exportation was absolutely forbidden, and sometimes it was a crime to introduce foreign corn into this country under any pretence whatever. There were long periods during which people were liable to be set in the pillory on conviction of the offence of buying corn in one market for the purpose of selling it in another within this country. The fact that those old Corn Laws constantly wanted mending, and were frequently being mended, is proof that they did not work very well. The law which. benefited the consumer very soon became a grievance to the producer; and when the producer procured a remedy, the consumer was in trouble and demanded relief. One thing is clear through the whole story : there never was a corn law which was quite satisfactory in its operation, while some of them have been more baneful than wars or famines.

In modern times the most tragic period in the history of the Corn Laws began with the ending of the great continental war, when Napoleon Bonaparte signed his abdication as Emperor of the French, and became the imprisoned monarch of the Island of St. Elba. A war of two or three years' duration between England and America came to an end about the same time.

It is necessary to explain the state of the Corn Laws for some thirty or forty years before the fall of Napoleon. By a law of 1773, so long as wheat was not more than 48s. per quarter the importation of foreign corn was forbidden. In 1791, avowedly in the interest of the owners of agricultural land, the importation of foreign corn was practically prohibited so long as English corn was less than 50s. a quarter. It was not actually forbidden, but what is called a "prohibitory duty" of 24s. 3d. was put upon foreign corn. If English corn, however, rose to 50s., there was a duty of only 2s. 6d. ; and while it was between 50s. and 54s. the duty was 6d. But the agriculturists were not yet satisfied ; and in 1804 a new Corn Law was passed, under which, so long as English corn was less than 63s. a quarter in the market, there was the prohibitory duty of 24s. 3d. a quarter on foreign corn, with small duties if the price rose higher.

The case then, at the time of the fall of Napoleon and at the end of the American War, reduced to its

simplest form, was that foreign corn could not come
into England so long as English wheat was under 63s.
a quarter, which would make bread and flour about
double the price at which those articles stood in the
winter of 1884-5. As a matter of fact, the prohibition
never came into operation between 1804 and 1814.
The price was so high during all that time that
foreign corn could be admitted under the law at 6d.
a quarter duty. During that time, the period of the
great war, farmers made fortunes quickly, and landowners had enormous rents for their land. When the
war ceased, and the seas and ports were free for commerce once again, great quantities of corn were
brought to England, attracted by high prices ; for in
1813 wheat was 106s. a quarter, and in 1812 it was
122s. (nearly four times the prices of the winter of
1884-5). The consequence of the great flood of foreign
corn was a large reduction in the price of wheat.
In the midst of the high prices during the war the
people were starving, and took to eating barley, rye
and oats ; as soon as the foreign corn came in with
the stoppage of the war, the farmers began to cry that
they would be ruined, for rents had been going up for
many years. What was to be done? Should the
landowners largely reduce their rents? Or should
a law be passed to keep up the price of corn, at
the expense of the poor people who wanted bread ?
Well, the poor people were not in Parliament to plead
their own cause against dear bread. Generally they

had no votes, and no voice in the election of members
of Parliament. So, in 1814, a Bill was introduced into
the House of Commons to prohibit the importation
of foreign corn until English corn reached a high
price. But the country was in a terrible state of
distress, and, in the face of very strong opposition in
and out of Parliament, the measure was withdrawn.
The question, however, was only postponed for a few
months, and in the early part of the year 1815 a Bill
was carried through Parliament practically prohibit-
ing the importation of corn until the price of wheat
in England should be as high as 80s. a quarter. The
following is Mr. Henry Ashworth's* account of the
manifestations of popular feeling against this measure:
" Whilst the legislature was engaged in the discussion
of this question, the people of London became riotous,
and the walls were chalked with invectives, such as
'Bread or Blood,' 'Guy Fawkes for ever,' &c. A
loaf, steeped in blood, was placed on Carlton House
(now the Carlton Club). The houses of some of the
most unpopular promoters of the measure were
attacked by the mob. At Lord Eldon's house the
iron railings were torn up, whilst every pane of glass
and many articles of furniture were broken and
destroyed, and it was facetiously remarked that his
lordship at last 'kept open house.' The military
were called out, and two persons were killed. The

* Recollections of Richard Cobden and the Anti-Corn-Law League,
by Henry Ashworth (Cassell & Company).

Houses of Parliament were guarded by soldiers, and, indeed, the whole of London appeared to be in possession of the army."

Similar disturbances prevailed in most of the populous districts of the North of England and the Midland counties.

In the course of the agitation and the rioting, the two questions of Free Trade in Corn and Parliamentary Reform were very much mixed up. People had grown hopeless of securing Free Trade in corn until there should be a different system of voting, and a different set of men sent to the House of Commons. In 1816, the double movement—for reform and cheap bread—grew very fierce, while 1817 was the year of the " Blanketeers."

The men of the agitation of 1817 were called " Blanketeers " because, having resolved to march to London in a body and lay their grievances before the Prince Regent, it was a part of their plan each to carry a blanket, or rug, in which to roll themselves up and sleep by the roadside, under the hedges, or in the fields by night, on their wretched journey from the North of England to the metropolis. They started from St. Peter's Field in Manchester on the 30th of March. But the authorities resolved not to allow them to find their way in this manner to London. The leaders of the movement were taken into custody and imprisoned. Troops held the roads between Manchester and the capital through

which the procession was to pass; and those of the
poor creatures who were not sent to prison were
dispersed.

Next came the "Battle of Peterloo." This was
in 1819. The House of Commons had refused to
take the subject of Reform into consideration. One
great meeting had been held in Manchester, at which
the cries were, "Universal Suffrage," and "No Corn
Laws." Similar meetings had been held at Birming-
ham, Leeds, and other places, and the Government
began to take measures to prevent these huge and
excited assemblies. The great Manchester meeting
of the 16th of August was arranged to be held in St.
Peter's Field—the spot on which stands now the
Free Trade Hall—lying at that time in the outskirts
of Manchester. Some 80,000 people were con-
gregated upon the field, carrying banners bearing
Reform and Anti-Corn-Law mottoes, and playing
bugles. Mr. "Orator Hunt," one of the popular leaders
of the time, was chairman, and spoke from a waggon.
While he was speaking, a body of mounted yeomanry,
with drawn swords, approached the waggon at a brisk
trot and seized Mr. Hunt as their prisoner. There
was much discussion afterwards on the question
whether or not the Riot Act was read, and whether
the people had been formally called upon to disperse;
but in any case the mass of the people knew nothing
of it. The crowd showed no signs of any intention
to disperse; somebody among the yeomanry cried

out, " Have at their flags ; " the mounted yeomanry
made a dash at the people, slashing about them with
their swords, and trampling them under their horses'
feet. It was very difficult for the people to escape,
on account of the density of the crowd, particularly
as the outlets were held by military detachments.
Some of the people threw stones and brickbats at the
yeomanry, but it was never alleged that any of them
suffered much injury. In the crowd eleven men,
women and children were killed, and six hundred
were wounded. It is said that from the coming up
of the yeomanry the whole attack did not last more
than ten minutes. The event soon after got the name
of the " Battle of Peterloo," and the records of the
Free Trade Hall at Manchester, erected in commemoration of the triumph, some seventeen years later,
of Richard Cobden and the Anti-Corn-Law League,
state that the building is erected on the site of the
" Massacre of Peterloo."

The event aroused a great deal of excitement in
the country. The bitterness of feeling among the
Reformers and Corn Law Repealers was much inten-
sified by the fact that the yeomanry were not soldiers,
but a body of volunteers consisting of farmers and
landowners, who were hence accused of cutting
and trampling down a starving people in the interest
of the high price of corn.

The agitation continued ; now subsiding a little
and now increasing, from the " Battle of Peterloo "

until the passing of the Reform Bill of 1832 ; but
in the interval, from various reasons, less was said
about the Corn Laws and more about Reform, and it
was reserved for the period after the Reform question
was for a time settled for a revival in full force of
the Free Trade movement.

Richard Cobden was a lad of fifteen when the
Battle of Peterloo was fought, just leaving his
wretched Yorkshire school and beginning life in
the warehouse at Old Change. After 1820 the price
of bread was generally lower, and the battle of
Reform was fought out more exclusively on its merits.
The Reform question, on its merits, as we have seen,
never moved Richard Cobden's mind so deeply as
did the fiscal question. It was when Free Trade
began to assume arge proportions among the
populace once again as a subject of agitation, after
1832, that Cobden began to be drawn into the
conflict.

What is called democratic representation was not
so much as begun in the Reform Act of 1832, and
it was not possible, except under extraordinary
conditions, to get, under that Act, a House of
Commons with a majority willing to carry out one
of the chief practical objects of the Reform Bill
agitation—the Repeal of the Corn Laws.

But the extraordinary conditions came after a
while. Fresh outbreaks of distress and want
among the poor, a revival with redoubled energy

of the old agitation against the Corn Laws, and the splendid leadership of this agitation by Richard Cobden, were the conditions.

It was, however, a long and fierce battle. By now it is universally allowed to have been the best and most ably managed popular movement in the history of political progress; and neither rival nor enemy, past nor present, has ever hesitated to admit that the agitation owed its success in the main to Richard Cobden, and that for such a task he was the ablest leader that has ever appeared upon the scene of English political life.

For the time the one burning question which had to be solved was—" How to get rid of the Corn Laws." In that question were the whole energy and resources of Richard Cobden's mind and character absorbed for the ten years or so which preceded the great triumph of his life in the Repeal of the duty on Corn.

It was not until after Cobden had produced his famous essay on "Russia," in 1836, and after he had been defeated, early in 1837, as a candidate for a seat in Parliament for the borough of Stockport, that he was impelled to make the Repeal of the Corn Laws the foremost, and for awhile the almost exclusive aim of his life as a public man.

The production of the pamphlet on " Russia," and his first Stockport electoral contest, are very interesting intermediate incidents in his career which must be briefly glanced at,

D

In 1836 there was a good deal of uneasiness in England, in and out of Parliament, respecting the long-standing quarrel between Russia and Turkey, which was threatening to break out into a war. Many English politicians contended that the rapidly increasing power of Russia was a danger to this country which should be somehow guarded against. We were, by means of war, alliances, and otherwise, to keep down Russia, and especially we were to prevent her from defeating and seizing upon Turkey. The Turkish Empire was to be maintained against its enemies, and particularly against Russia, in order to preserve the "balance of power" in Europe. All these views as to the danger of the increasing power of Russia, as to the necessity of keeping the Turkish Empire from falling and preventing it from passing into the hands of the Czar, and as to what Cobden regarded as the mischievous superstition of the "balance of power," he challenged, with quite wonderful force, cogency, and ability, in this pamphlet, and the essay had a very great effect upon the political controversy of the hour. "Even if Russia were to subjugate Turkey," said Cobden in his essay, "England would gain rather than suffer by the event."

After describing the beauty, richness, and fertility of the country ruled by the Turks, who, he reminds his readers, are "a race of Tartars of Asia," he says: "The Turks profess, as is well known, the most bigoted and intolerant branch of the Mahometan faith; they regard with equal detestation the Persian Shiite and the follower of Christ; nay, the more zealous amongst their doctors contend that it is as meritorious to slay one Shiite as twenty Christians. Their colleges, or madresses, teach nothing but the Mahometan theology, many years being spent in mastering such knotty points as whether the feet should be washed at rising, or only rubbed with the dry hand.

"Such an example," he adds, "as a Turkish merchant transacting matters of commerce with a foreign trader was scarcely ever known in that country."

While he was publishing anonymously these at that time quite fresh and novel views of national policy, he had become pretty widely known among the Reformers and Free Traders of Lancashire. The first record that is found of his personal activity in public affairs relates to his efforts in connection with others to establish a school for poor children at Sabden, in "the once lonely valleys and wild moors of East Lancashire." His first speech attempted before an audience of politicians and public men was in 1835, at a meeting on the question of the establishment of a municipal Corporation for Manchester; for, until the Reform Act of 1832, Manchester was, in the eye of the law, simply a monstrous and densely populated village. It needs a sensitive and keen temperament to make a great speaker. This man, the author of "England, Ireland, and America," the man

who, only a very few years later, became one of
the most accomplished debaters in the House of
Commons, was nervous and diffident in rising to
address his fellow-citizens in the cotton capital, and
his speech is reported to have been a failure.

Very soon, however, he became known all over
that quarter of England as a good speaker, and a very
earnest and effective advocate on questions of political
and social progress which engaged his interest. It is
of this period that Mr. John Bright spoke, only a few
years ago, to an audience in Bradford, on the occasion
of the unveiling of the Cobden statue in that town,
in giving an account of his first meeting with his
friend Richard Cobden. He said :—" The first time I
became acquainted with him was in connection
with the subject of education. I went over to Manchester to call upon him, to ask him if he would be
kind enough to come to Rochdale, and to speak at an
education meeting which was about to be held in the
schoolroom in the Baptist Chapel in West Street in
that town. I found him in his office in Morley
Street. I introduced myself to him. I told him what
I wanted. His countenance lit up with pleasure to
find that there were others that were working in this
question, and he, without hesitation, agreed to come.
He came, and he spoke ; and though he was then so
young as a speaker, yet the qualities of his speech
were such as remained with him so long as he was
able to speak at all—clearness, logic, a conversational

eloquence, a persuasiveness which, when conjoined
with the absolute truth which there was in his eye and
in his countenance—a persuasiveness which it was
almost impossible to resist."

It was about this time that he travelled for a few
months in the East for his health's sake, and on his
return to Lancashire, in 1837, he found himself a candidate for Stockport at the general election. In the
election Free Trade was only one of the questions on
the Liberal programme at Stockport, and it was not
the predominant question. It was and is a town of
factories, and a question in which the people took
great interest was factory legislation. On this
question Cobden pronounced his clear opinion—first
that factory work for children ought to be restricted by
law,* and secondly that the law ought not to interfere
with the liberty of adult work-people as to the hours
and the regulation of labour. He lost the election,
but he fought it with so much earnestness and ability
as to make a remarkable impression on the Reformers
of the borough, particularly among the non-electors.
After the election he was so popular that tradesmen
stuck placards in their shop windows, inscribed " Voted
for Cobden," and in the market-place the salesmen

* " In my opinion," said Cobden—" and I hope to see the day
when such a feeling is universal—no child ought to be put to
work in a cotton mill at all so early as the age of thirteen
years ; and after that the hours should be moderate and the
labour light."

cried their wares as "Cobden beef," "Cobden potatoes," and the like. And though only 418 electors voted for him, seventeen thousand persons subscribed a penny each to present him with a piece of plate in commemoration of the contest. At the presentation Cobden was accompanied by the great Daniel O'Connell, who was an eloquent advocate of Free Trade, and the speeches were made at a vast open-air meeting. Cobden, having just passed through his first personal experience at an election, devoted the greater part of his address to the question of "vote by ballot." Unless they got secret voting, he contended, household suffrage, the repeal of the Corn Laws, and the shortening of Parliaments would be insecure benefits. It had been made evident to him that a considerable number of the electors of Stockport dared not vote in accordance with their own wishes and principles.

But that election, though he failed, gave the final turn to his career. He resolved at once to make such arrangements as to his business as to leave the way open to him to devote his time and energies henceforth to politics. It was within the same year, and not long after the Stockport election, that the course of events and the turn of public opinion convinced him that the question of questions from that time forth should be the Repeal of the Corn Laws.

CHAPTER VII.

THE ANTI-CORN-LAW LEAGUE.

CONSPICUOUS in the movements in Lancashire on behalf of Reform and Free Trade, during the period of some thirty or forty years immediately preceding the Repeal of the Corn Laws, was Mr. Archibald Prentice, proprietor and editor of the *Manchester Times*, who has perhaps a better title than any other man to the credit of originating the organisation in Manchester which presently developed into the Anti-Corn-Law League. Some years afterwards he wrote the "History of the Anti-Corn-Law League," and in that work he gives an account of the beginning of his acquaintance with Richard Cobden which affords a very interesting glimpse of the manner and bearing of the man, then almost unknown, who was soon to be recognised as the master spirit of the Free Trade movement. Mr. Prentice, after telling how greatly the cause of Free Trade in corn stood in need of a new man with gifts for the popular championship of the cause such as were not possessed by any one then engaged in the movement, brings us face to face with Cobden in the following passage :—" In 1835 there had been sent to me for publication in my paper some admirably written letters. They contained no internal evidence to guide me in guessing as to who might be the writer, and I concluded that there was some new man amongst us who, if he held a station that would enable him to take a part in public affairs, would exert a widely beneficial influence amongst us. . . . I told many that a new man had come, and the question was often put among my friends, 'Who is he?' In the course of that year (1835), a pamphlet, published under the title, 'England, Ireland, and America,' was put into my hand by a friend, inscribed, "From the author," and I instantly recognised the handwriting of my unknown correspondent; and I was greatly gratified when I learnt that Mr. Cobden, the author of the pamphlet, desired to meet me at my friend's house. I went with something of the same kind of feeling which I had experienced when I first, four years before, went to visit Jeremy Bentham, the father of the practical Free Traders. Nor was I disappointed, except in one respect. I found a man who could enlighten by his knowledge, counsel by his prudence, and conciliate by his temper and manners; and who, if he found his way into the House of Commons, would secure its respectful attention; but I had been an actor amongst men who from 1812 to 1832 had fought in the rough battle for Parliamentary Reform, and I missed, in the unassuming gentleman before me, not the energy, but the apparent hardihood and dash which I had, forgetting the change of times, believed to be requisites to the success of a popular leader. In after

years, and after having attained great platform popu-
larity, he had been elected a member of Parliament,
and when men sneered and said he would soon
find his level there, as other mob orators had done, I
ventured to say that he would be in his proper voca-
tion there, and that his level would be amongst the first
men in the House. From the time that Cobden made
his public appearance in print in the year 1835, I
did not hesitate publicly to declare my strong conviction that any Lancashire borough would do itself
honour by returning him as its representative to Parliament."

Mr. Henry Ashworth relates* that in the autumn
of 1837 he and Mr. Cobden were attending the annual
meeting of the British Association at Liverpool.
They were both members of the Manchester
Chamber of Commerce, and in the course of their
talk on the political questions of the time the
necessity for the Repeal of the Corn Laws became
a constant subject of conversation. "One evening,"
says Mr. Ashworth, "after a *soirée* at the Liverpool
Town Hall, Cobden stopped suddenly as we were
walking quietly at midnight up Pembroke Place, and
with some abruptness said : "I'll tell you what we
will do ; we'll use the Chamber of Commerce for an
agitation to repeal the Corn Laws." There seemed
to be some difficulty in the way of this scheme, but
Cobden presently declared that he was determined to

* " Recollections of Cobden and the League."

put forth his strength for the repeal of the Corn and Provision Laws.

The following year was a year of distress and trouble in the land. The Chartist agitation had begun to grow violent. The Chartists were the more advanced Reformers who were not satisfied with the Reform Act of 1832, and they began their movement soon after the passing of that Act. They wanted a vote for every man, a general election every year, vote by ballot, the payment of members of Parliament for their services, the division of the country into equal districts for representation in Parliament, and the abolition of the property qualification of members. In the time of distress in 1838 they held torchlight meetings, and became riotous. They wanted the repeal of the Corn Laws, and many other reforms, but they did not believe that any of these things would be accomplished by a Parliament elected by ten-pound voters in boroughs and fifty-pound voters in the counties. They were therefore impatient with the Free Trade movement, and often opposed it, insisting that the only possible way of securing the Repeal of the Corn Laws was by demanding the reform of Parliament on the Chartist plan.

A terrible time seemed to be coming again, of which Mr. Morley speaks thus: " The price of wheat had risen to seventy-seven shillings in August ; there was every prospect of a wet harvesting ; the revenue was declining; deficit was becoming a familiar word; pauperism was increasing; and the manufacturing population of Lancashire were finding it impossible to support themselves, because the landlords, and the legislation of a generation of landlords before them, insisted on keeping the first necessity of life at an artificially high rate."

Writing on the subject of these disturbances, Cobden expressed the hope that these "scattered elements" might yet be "rallied round the question of the Corn Laws," which he thought could be made irresistible if it were agitated in the same manner in which the question of slavery had been agitated.

A meeting of seven men was held in October in Manchester, and an Anti-Corn-Law Association was formed. Cobden and others at once joined the band, and this was the foundation of the League. In December the very thing was attempted which Cobden had suggested to Mr. Ashworth at Liverpool. A meeting was convened of the Manchester Chamber of Commerce, to consider the effect of the Corn Laws. The president, Mr. Wood, M.P. for Kendal, was for moderate measures. He favoured a petition to Parliament to *reduce* the duty on corn. Cobden and the members of the Anti-Corn-Law Association were for total repeal. The question was discussed for some hours. "Cobden," says Mr. Morley, "struck into the debate with that finely tempered weapon of argumentative speech which was his most singular endowment. The turbid sediment of miscellaneous discussion sank away, as he brought out a lucid proof that the Corn Law was the only obstacle to a vast increase of their trade, and that every shilling of the protection on corn which then obstructed their prosperity passed into the pockets of the landowners, without conferring an atom of advantage on the farmer or the labourer.

The discussion was not ripe for ending, and the proceedings were adjourned for a week. In those seven days Mr. Cobden, Mr. Ashworth, and others prepared another memorial praying for "the repeal of all laws relating to the importation of foreign corn and other foreign articles of subsistence." Cobden was the mover of this petition. It was discussed for five hours. The petition set forth that the duty on corn prevented the British manufacturer from exchanging the produce of his labour for the corn of other countries, and so enabled his foreign rivals to purchase their food at half the price at which it was sold in the English market. It was a memorial to the Houses of Parliament to apply the principle of Free Trade at once to agriculture and to manufactures. The document bears upon it the stamp of Cobden's point of view and forms of expression. He was successful. The petition was adopted by an overwhelming majority, and the President of the Chamber of Commerce resigned.

Richard Cobden was now the master-spirit of the

movement. Under his advice the Anti-Corn-Law Association set to work to raise a fund, and in a month more than six thousand pounds was subscribed. A great Free Trade banquet was held. On the day after the feast Mr. Cobden met a number of delegates from various towns, and explained to them his scheme for the formation of local Anti-Corn-Law Associations in different centres of population, to be all united in one centre at Manchester.

That is how the Anti-Corn-Law League was initiated in the early days of 1839. It was not many weeks before the plan took a very practical and effective shape in the greatest and most famous organisation for political agitation that the world has ever seen. Some able and enthusiastic men were associated with Mr. Cobden in the work. Mr. Prentice had said in his paper: "There ought to be a systematic opposition to the continuance of the Bread Tax; let half a dozen persons in each of the surrounding towns meet together, and resolve to agitate the question in public meetings; the matter only needs a beginning."

It had a good beginning. In the first Provisional Committee of the Anti-Corn-Law Association appeared the name of Mr. John Bright, who was to labour so hard with Cobden, and with such wonderful effect, in the cause. Another name on that first list was Thomas Potter (afterwards Sir Thomas), father of Mr. Thomas Bayley Potter, M.P., the founder, in 1866, of the Cobden Club.

Mr. A. W. Paulton, a young medical student, was the leading lecturer in connection with the movement. Dr. Bowring (afterwards Sir John Bowring) was among the foremost of the band to denounce the Corn Laws from the public platform in Manchester. The original Executive Committee of the Association consisted of twelve men ; and when the work of the League was completed, seven years later, and the League was dissolved, these were the remaining six on that committee, which had been changed into the Council of the Anti-Corn-Law League : Richard Cobden, Archibald Prentice, George Wilson, W. R. Callender, William Evans, and William Rawson.

CHAPTER VIII.

INSTRUCTING THE NATION.

THE task of the Anti-Corn-Law League, Mr. Cobden said, was to be that of "instructing the nation." There had been agitations of the starving poor for cheap bread ; but the starving poor had no votes, no system, no persistence, no clear grasp of the soundness of the principle of Free Trade, and no means of bringing conviction home to the minds of those who held the power in their hands. Cobden's League set to work "to obtain by all legal and constitutional means, such as the formation of local associations, the delivery of lectures, the distribution of tracts, and the presentation of petitions to Parliament—the total and immediate Repeal of the Corn and Provision Laws."

There was a period of only two years between the commencement of the League's work and the beginning of Cobden's great career as a member of Parliament. The two years were spent in the work of arousing the country to a sense of the importance of this question, and in the constant attempt to influence the House of Commons and the Government in favour of the Repeal of the Corn Laws. The League was most liberally supported with money by the great manufacturers and merchants of Lancashire and the North of England. Meetings were held in the large towns up and down the country, at which Cobden soon became the best known and the most popular of the speakers. His mode of address was simple and natural. It was the very perfection of the conversational style of address. He was not in the habit of indulging in grand flights of oratory, but he was one of the most persuasive and convincing speakers that the world has seen. " So cogent and exhaustive was Cobden's reasoning," says Mr. Thorold Rogers, "that in almost every case they who attempted to resist the effect of his conclusions were constrained to betake themselves to some irrelevant issue, or to awaken some prejudice against him. What he said, too, was stated with great

geniality and kindliness. If it was difficult to refute
the speaker, it was impossible to quarrel with the
man. He was as popular as he was wise. His
manner was as modest as his speech was lucid."

Cobden and his partners in this great agitation
did not meet with much encouragement from the
statesmen of the time. " I remember right well,"
said he, looking back to this period, in a speech
which he made some years later, " when we came
to London six years ago, in the spring of 1839,
there were three of us in a small room at Brown's
Hotel, in Palace Yard ; we were visited by a nobleman, one who had taken an active part in the
modification of the Corn Laws but not the total
Repeal ; he asked us, 'What is it that has brought
you to town, and what do you come to seek ?' We
said, ' We come to seek the total and immediate
Repeal of the Corn Laws.' The nobleman said, with
an emphatic shake of the head, 'You will overturn
the monarchy as soon as you will accomplish that.'"

In that same spring some 200 delegates from
various districts met in London, and waited upon
the Prime Minister, Lord Melbourne. The noble
lord was at the head of a Liberal administration, but,
when the deputation explained to him that their
object was the Repeal of the Corn Laws, he replied :
"You know that to be impracticable."

Only seven years before the total Repeal of the
Corn Laws the men who agitated for the Repeal

were looked upon, by many of the most experienced statesmen of · the country, as wild and reckless theorists—as, in fact, little better than madmen !

Before that deputation left London they had interviews with Sir Robert Peel, the leader of the Conservative Party, and with Sir James Graham. Sir Robert Peel gave them no hope. Sir James Graham had no patience with the delegates or their arguments, and when Mr. Henry Ashworth submitted that it was grossly unjust to restrict the imports of food in order to uphold the rents of farming land, and declared that the effect would be to increase the sense of unfair treatment which was felt by the people, Sir James stopped him with the exclamation, "Why, you are a leveller !" and asked, "Am I to infer that the labouring classes have some claim to the landlords' estates?" Presently Sir James, in reply to the whole case which had been laid before him, asserted that if the Corn Laws were repealed, great disasters would fall upon the country, the land would go out of cultivation ; Church and State could not be upheld! all our institutions would be reduced to their primitive elements, and the people whom the Corn Law Repealers were exciting would pull down our houses about our ears. Such was the language of statesmen whom Mr. Cobden was destined to convert to the doctrine of Free Trade in corn in less than seven years.

E

There was one great champion of Free Trade in
the House of Commons, Mr. Charles P. Villiers, the
member for Wolverhampton, who, at the age of 83, is
still (1885) a member of the House, having represented the borough of Wolverhampton for more than
half a century.   In those years of the agitation of the
Anti-Corn-Law League Mr. Villiers introduced every
year in the House a motion " That the House should
resolve itself into a committee to take into consideration the Act regulating the importation of foreign
corn."   In the early part of the session of 1839 he
moved that a number of petitions against the Corn
Laws should be referred to a committee of the whole
House.   Those were mainly the petitions which came
from the movements of the League, and in the
wording of many of them might be seen the point,
the argument, the marshalling of facts which marked
the hand of Richard Cobden.   The House rejected
the motion.   Then Mr. Villiers moved that certain
members of the Manchester Anti-Corn-Law Association should be heard at the bar.   The motion was
defeated by 361 votes against 172.   The delegates,
waiting in London for the decision of the House, met
the next morning to consider what should be their next
step.   There was no sign of discouragement.   Richard
Cobden was there.   He was the spirit, the vigour,
the inspiration of the movement.   He had devoted
himself, without any secondary purpose or reserva-
tion of interest in any other object, public or private,

to the one task of "instructing the nation." Speaking
to his brother delegates on the decision of the House
of Commons, he said : "The delegates have offered
to instruct the House ; the House has refused to
be instructed ; and the most unexceptionable and
effectual way will be by instructing the nation."

In about a couple of weeks after the utterance of
that declaration, on the 7th of March, 1839, the
delegates were summoned to a great meeting in
Manchester. Among the large towns represented
at that meeting were Liverpool, Manchester, Bir-
mingham, Glasgow, London, Leeds, Bolton, Derby,
Burnley, Dundee, Leicester, Lancaster, Huddersfield,
Hull, Edinburgh, Bradford, Nottingham, Kendal,
Wigan, Warrington, Sowerby Bridge. It was then
resolved to meet at Brown's Hotel, Palace Yard, on
the 12th of March, that being the day on which Mr.
Villiers was to bring on his motion calling upon the
House in committee " to take into consideration the
Act 9 George IV. regulating the importation of
foreign corn."

The delegates met in Palace Yard again and
again, for the motion was discussed for five nights.
As yet Cobden's time had not quite come for playing
his great part in the debates on the question on the
floor of the House of Commons, but he was a power
of hopefulness and of intellectual and moral resources
among the delegates, who, from the 'vantage-ground
of Brown's Hotel, watched the legislature from day to

day in that memorable week—the week which gave
to the new League the impulse that it wanted for its
splendid enterprise. At length the House came to
the vote, and Mr. Villiers' motion was defeated by
the decisive majority of 147, the numbers being 342
against 195.

Not until then had Cobden's scheme for the
establishing of the League assumed its final, definite,
practical shape. The delegates held one more
meeting in London before they departed from under
the shadow of the hostile House of Commons. There
was some despondency among them, but, says Mr.
Morley, "the greater part almost instantly came
round to the energetic mind of Cobden; he recalled
the delegates to the fact that, in spite of the House
over the way, they represented three millions of the
people; he compared the alliance of the great towns
of England to the League of the Hanse towns of
Germany; that League had turned the castles which
crowned the rocks along the Rhine, the Danube, and
the Elbe into dismantled memorials of the past, and
the new League would not fail in dismantling the
legislative stronghold of the new feudal oppressors of
England."

It was when things had arrived at this pass that
all the local Anti-Corn-Law associations were brought
into the union which was to be known as the League;
and it was then that the executive committee of the
Manchester Association were duly constituted the

Council of the Anti-Corn-Law League. Manchester became the centre or head-quarters of the League, and hence it came about, in the course of political controversy, that Cobden and those who acted with him, in and out of Parliament, were described as the " Manchester School " of politicians.

The name was understood to signify not simply that these men were Free Traders, but that they were a political party who regarded all, or nearly all, political questions from the point of view of the interests of trade or manufacture.

Then the serious business of "instructing the nation " began. The demand of starving thousands for cheap bread had been heard often enough in times of stress and trial; but they who understood the question of Free Trade, either as a principle or in its application to the complicated conditions of industry and commerce, were few, whether among poor or rich, the educated or the ignorant. It was the business of the League to make the country comprehend the rights of the question, and this task was carried out with splendid energy and ability, and at a vast cost. A periodical paper, the *Anti-Corn-Law Circular*, the organ of the League, was started for the dissemination of information and argument on the great question ; tracts, leaflets, and pamphlets were distributed by hundreds of thousands; lecturers were sent up and down the country ; meetings were called, both in large towns and in country districts, at which in many cases Cobden, or some other well-qualified spokesman of the League, would be present.

To measure or describe the progress of the movement would be very difficult. The agitators found the first year's work very hard. The people had been in the habit of making their wants and miseries known from time to time by demonstrations which were, according to circumstances, either feared or ridiculed by steady-going citizens. The Reform Bill had been carried by force of the peril of a revolution. The country had not been accustomed up to that time to expect to move Parliament by argument at public meetings—by, in fact, what is now called the movement of public opinion. Up to half a century ago what few reforms were passed in Parliament were in the main due to an impulse of wisdom—and of a desire for the remedy of grievances—in the minds of some members of Parliament gifted with faculties and tendencies of mind above the common level. Speaking in a broad and general sense, the modern system of government, legislation, and administration, very largely influenced by public opinion—by the pressure of the evident sense and feeling of the country—began with the Anti-Corn-Law League ; and Cobden and the disciples of the League found for a time that they had a very hard task to perform.

In carrying the movement into districts new to any sort of agitation on questions of this kind, the League spokesmen and lecturers reported that they got a more temperate hearing and better acceptance in Scotland than in England.

In some parts of England the lecturers encountered great hostility. Here are a few incidents mentioned by Mr. Morley.

At Arundel the mayor refused the use of the town hall, as he said that the effect of the discussion would be to make the labourers discontented. The landlord of the hotel refused the use of his large room, saying that it would offend his customers. A farmer, who owned land, offered a bushel of wheat to anybody who would throw the lecturer into the river.

At Petersfield the Free Trade lecturer, when he had delivered his address and gone back to his inn, where he had ordered tea and a bed, was turned out of the house by the landlord and landlady.

At Louth the lecturers were refused the use of the public hall on the second night of their appearance, and had to speak from a gig in the market-place; they were then summoned for causing an obstruction in a public thoroughfare, and fined by a magistrate who had engaged in discussion with one of the lecturers on the first night.

At Stamford they had to encounter a mob who threatened to tear them to pieces.

The histories and contemporary records of the League abound with examples of the extraordinary battle which Cobden and his friends had to fight from end to end of the country; but the agitation supplied the League with abundant evidence of the misery which existed among the poor in consequence of the corn duty, and with satisfactory proof that there was almost everywhere a thoughtful section of the population whose minds were deeply affected by the arguments and facts which were brought under their attention.

Another branch of the work of Cobden and the League is thus referred to by Mr. Morley: "Enormous masses of material for the case (of the Repeal of the Corn Laws) poured every week into the offices of the League. All day long Cobden was talking with men who had something to tell him. Correspondents from every quarter of the land plied him with information. Yet he was never overwhelmed by the volume of the stream. He was incessantly on the alert for a useful fact, a telling illustration, a new fallacy to expose. So dexterously did he move through the ever-growing piles of matter that it seemed to his companions as if nothing apposite ever escaped him, and nothing irrelevant ever detained him."

Mr. Cobden, Mr. Bright, Colonel Perronet Thompson, Mr. Ashworth, and other well-known spokesmen of the League, delivered addresses during these years in nearly every town in England and Scotland. Gigantic meetings were held in Manchester, and in London. The following is Mr. Morley's description of the incidents and effects of Mr. Cobden's arguments in the campaign of the League in the rural districts, where, as a general rule, the farmers were strongly prejudiced in favour of the Corn Laws : " Farmers who were afraid of attending meetings in their own immediate district, used to travel thirty or forty miles to places where they could listen to the speakers without being known. Enemies came to the meetings, and began to take notes in a very confident spirit, but as the arguments became too strong for them the pencil was laid aside and the paper was torn up. At Norwich the leading yeomen of the county put a number of questions to Cobden, which were so neatly and conclusively answered that the farmers who were listening to the controversy burst out into loud applause."

Here is another incident as given in Mr. Morley's Life of Cobden : " At Uxbridge the farmers who usually attended the corn-market invited Cobden to explain his views to them. The arrangements for the meeting were left entirely in their own hands. The tickets of admission were issued by the farmers, and disposed of by them ; the county was ransacked for supporters of the Corn Law monopoly, and the discomfiture of the prophet of the League was confidently predicted. The audience was more exclusively composed of farmers than any which had yet been held. When the time came, four gentlemen, one after another, advocated the cause of monopoly

as ably as they could, and the discussion between
them on the one hand and Cobden and Joseph
Hume on the other lasted for four hours and a half.
In the end the arguments of the Free Traders were
held to be so absolutely unanswerable that a resolution in favour of total and immediate Repeal was
carried by five to one.

A similar result followed a similar meeting at
Lincoln, when Cobden and John Bright were the
principal speakers, and "at Taunton the church bells
were rung, flags with Free-Trade mottoes were hung
from the windows, and a brass band insisted upon
accompanying the deputation from the railway to the
place of meeting. Cobden, Mr. Bright, and Mr. Moore
were listened to with unwearied attention for more
than four hours. The farmers listened at first with
doubt and suspicion. Gradually their faces cleared,
conviction began to warm them, and at last such an
impression had been made that eight hundred
farmers out of a meeting of twelve hundred persons
voted in favour of total and immediate Repeal"

Another example may be quoted from Mr.
Morley's book of the surprising effect of Cobden's
advocacy of Repeal upon rural assemblies strongly
predisposed against the movement: "In Bedford
Cobden had not a single friend or acquaintance. He
had simply announced as extensively as he could by
placards, that he meant to visit the town on a given
day. The farmers had been canvassed far and wide

to attend to put down the representatives from the Anti-Corn-Law League. The Assembly Rooms could not hold half the persons who had come together, and they adjourned to a large field outside the town. Three waggons were provided to serve as hustings, but the monopolist party rudely seized them, and Cobden had to wait while a fourth waggon was procured. Lord Charles Russell presided, and the discussion began. The proceedings went on from three in the afternoon until nine o'clock in the evening, in spite of heavy showers of rain. At first Cobden was listened to with some impatience, but as he warmed to his subject, and began to deliver telling strokes of illustration and argument, the impression gradually spread that he was right," and the amendment in favour of Free Trade was carried by a large majority.

"After Bedford we can win anywhere," wrote Cobden to his brother, "and it is giving great moral power to my movements in the rural districts to be *always* successful."

The greatest of these victories, Mr. Morley tells us, was at Colchester: "The whole district had been astir with angry expectation for many days. Passions waxed very high; special constables were sworn in; and the violent and the timid alike declared that the agitators would find themselves in no small bodily peril. Hustings were erected in a large field, and when the day came several thousands of people assembled from all parts of the country. At the appointed hour Cobden and Charles Villiers were at their posts, and they were soon followed by Sir Charles Tyrrell and Mr. Ferrand (great opponents of Repeal). Then the tournament began. The battle raged for six hours, and the League champion achieved a striking victory. The amendment to the resolution was put to utter rout, and when night fell Sir John Tyrrell was found to have silently vanished. At one point in the controversy he had irreverently defied Cobden to do further battle with him at Chelmsford. Cobden instantly took up the glove, and on the appointed day to Chelmsford he went. Sir John, however, had already had enough of the unequal match, and Cobden carried on the controversy in the usual way, and with the usual success."

These rural meetings, with their rustic assemblies, were splendidly relieved, in the spectacle of this stupendous agitation, by the gigantic and enthusiastic Free Trade meetings in Drury Lane and Covent Garden theatres, and in Manchester and all the great towns and cities. It is not too much to say that at times the whole attention of the country was fixed upon the figure of Richard Cobden, delivering those most persuasive, irrefutable, and convincing practical speeches, full of argument and illustration, which brought the abstract conclusions of political economy within range of the understanding of all classes and conditions of people.

The agitation was carried on, varying in tone and character, and in its effects upon the public mind—according to the changing price of corn, to the condition of industry, and to the fortunes of the question in Parliament—from the establishment of the League until the final triumph of the cause. But one most important event divides the period almost into two equal parts. That event is the return of Cobden to Parliament as member for Stockport.

CHAPTER IX.

COBDEN IN PARLIAMENT.

THERE was a dissolution of Parliament at Midsummer, 1841. Powerful as was the opposition in the House of Commons to the Repeal of the Corn Laws, the Free Trade question, in one form or another, kept Ministers and parties in constant trouble. Less than three years of the Anti-Corn-Law League, with Richard Cobden at its head, seemed to have rendered it impossible for any Government to get a settled and peaceful tenure of office. Without having ever had a seat in Parliament Cobden may be said to have caused the downfall of Lord Melbourne's administration.

He was a candidate again for Stockport, and he

won easily. Several other League candidates won
seats in northern constituencies. But this was only
the beginning of the great task in Parliament. There
was found to be in the House of Commons a majority
of ninety-one for Sir Robert Peel, the great Conservative leader. A very strong Government was formed
with Peel for Prime Minister. There were yet only
ninety members in the House in favour of the total
repeal of the Corn Laws. On the re-appearance of the
annual motion of Mr. Villiers it was rejected by
393 to 90, a majority of 303 against the repeal.
This was the stupendous majority which Cobden and
Villiers and the League had to do battle with, and it
was broken down in about five years !

The story of the successive debates in Parliament
during these five years—the conflict over questions of
a fixed duty or a sliding scale, the state of feeling in
the country, the depression and dear bread and bad
harvests, the incessant agitation by the League
outside the walls of Parliament—is a very long story
indeed, which must be read in the pages of the
political and social history of the time. In this
chapter we must be content with glimpses of Richard
Cobden, now in the debates on the floor of the House
of Commons, and now addressing great crowds in
London and the provinces.

His first speech in Parliament commanded exceptional attention, and was the talk of the country
when the reports appeared in the newspapers. It was

in the debate on the first meeting of the new House after the General Election—the debate which turned out Lord Melbourne and put Sir Robert Peel in office. Of this speech Mr. Morley says : " It sounded a new key, and startled men by an accent that was strange in the House of Commons ; the thoughtful among them recognising the rare tone of reality, and the note of a man dealing with things and not words. He produced that singular and profound effect which is perceived in English deliberative assemblies when a speaker leaves party recriminations, abstract argument, and commonplaces of sentiment, in order to inform his hearers of telling facts in the condition of the nation. Cobden reminded the House that it was the condition of the nation, and not the interest of a class or the abstract doctrines of the economist, that cried for a relief which it was in the power of the legislature to bestow. This was the point of the speech. In spite of the strong wish of everybody on the side of the majority, and of many on the side of the minority, to keep the Corn Law out of the debate, Cobden insisted that the Corn Law was in reality the only matter which at that moment was worth debating at all. The family of a nobleman, he showed the House, paid to the bread tax about one halfpenny on every hundred pounds of income, while the effect of the tax on the family of the labouring man was not less than twenty per cent."

In this speech, as in many another made in the

House and in the country, Cobden set himself to the exposure of the fallacy—upheld by the Protectionists in England then as it is upheld by the Protectionists of the United States to-day—that Protection and high prices increase the wages of workmen and labourers. Speaking of the agricultural labourers, Cobden said: "These unfortunate men are told that their wages will rise as the price of provision advances. Why? Is it because the high price of provisions increases the demand for labour, or is it from pure charity? . . . The rate of wages has no more connection with the price of food than with the moon's changes."

He turned to the same point in his second speech in the House, upon the annual motion of Mr. Villiers. Referring to the debates, which he had been reading, of 1814, when the first stringent Corn Law was passed, he said he found that all the speakers on all sides, at that time, were under the erroneous impression that the price of food regulated the rate of wages. "In reading the debates of that date," he said, "I have been filled with the deepest sorrow to find how those who passed that measure were deluded; but," he added, "there was one party, that most interested, the working classes, who were not deluded. The great multitude of the nation, without the aid of learning, saw with that intuitive and instructive sagacity which has given rise to the adage, 'The voice of the people is the voice of God,' what the effect of the measure would be upon wages; and therefore it was, that when that law was passed, this House was surrounded by the multitudes of London, whom you were compelled to keep from your doors by the point of the bayonet. Yes; and no sooner was the law passed than there arose disturbances and tumults everywhere, and in London bloodshed and murder ensued : for a coroner's jury returned a verdict of wilful murder against the soldiers who were called out and fired upon the people."

There was, however, he insisted, not the same excuse in 1841 for maintaining this fallacy about the price of food and the rate of wages that there was in 1815, and he ventured to say he firmly believed that if the members of the House in 1815 had been cognizant of the facts now before the House they would never have passed that Corn Bill. And this is how Cobden addressed the House upon the point: " If one thing is more surprising than others in the facts which I have mentioned, it is to find in this House, where lecturers of all things in the world are so much decried, the ignorance which prevails on this question amongst honourable members on the other side of the House [Oh ! oh !]. Yes, I have never seen their ignorance equalled amongst any equal number of working men in the north of England. Do you think that the fallacy of 1815, which I heard put forth so boldly last week, that wages rose and fell with the price of bread, can now prevail in the minds of working men after the experience of the last three years ?

F

Has not the price of bread been higher during that time than for any three consecutive years for the last twenty years ? And yet trade has suffered a greater decline in every branch of industry than in any preceding three years."

It is a note of no mean historic importance that, some years after this speech was delivered, Sir Robert Peel confessed that he had accepted without proper examination the economic fallacy which Cobden herein exposed. Men of a smaller quality of mind than Peel might hug the mistake they had made in spite of Cobden's unanswerable exposure of it, but to Peel's mind the conviction was driven home that the price of corn did not rule the price of labour, and that, in fact, when corn was dearest wages might be at the lowest ; and that seems to have been the beginning of the conversion of the Prime Minister to the doctrine of the League.

In another of his earliest speeches in the House Cobden used one of his favourite forms of illustration of the absurdity of setting up a tariff barrier against trade between one country and another. This is how he put it, speaking of the duty on corn and other produce between England and the United States: "Suppose now that it was but the Thames instead of the Atlantic which separated the two countries; suppose that the people on one side were mechanics and artisans, capable by their industry of producing a vast supply of manufactures, and that the people on

the other side were agriculturists, producing infinitely
more than they could themselves consume of corn,
pork and beef—fáncy these two separate peoples
anxious and willing to exchange with each other the
produce of their common industries, and fancy a
demon rising from the middle of the river—for I
cannot imagine anything human in such a position
and performing such an office—fancy a demon rising
from the river and holding in his hand an Act of
Parliament, and saying, 'You shall not supply each
other's wants,' and then in addition to that, let it be
supposed that this demon said to his victim with an
affected smile, 'This is for your benefit; I do it
entirely for your protection.'"

"Where," asked Cobden, turning round to the
champions of the tariff fallacy, "where is the difference
between the Thames and the Atlantic?"

It is a rare lesson in the study of political history
to watch this man, coming forth from the midst of
the people outside Parliament, fresh from the study
of Adam Smith on the one side and of the actual
state of the country on the other, and making a
mockery thus of the fine, false theoretic fancies of the
men of the great ruling classes who regarded themselves as practical politicians.

It had been said that Richard Cobden, the Anti-
Corn-Law Leaguer, would soon "find his level" in
the House of Commons. He found his level indeed;
and men who had graduated in statesmanship for

a generation or two found their level when they had him face to face with them. It is said, and with some truth no doubt, that speakers in Parliament, however eloquent and however forcible in argument, do not often produce a great change of opinion in those who listen to them. But Cobden carried from his study of books, and men, and trade, and labour outside, a new atmosphere of thought, and a new point of view, fresh as it were from nature, into the House; and there happened a phenomenon rare, and perhaps wholly unexampled in the history of Parliament. He carried the House of Commons over to his side of the question. Not at once; but it was the same House of Commons, the same Government, the same Prime Minister who sat and listened in 1841 to the remarks we have just quoted. There was no General Election between the day when Cobden made his first speech on the floor of the House and the day, five years later, when Sir Robert Peel got up and astonished the world by the announcement of a measure for the repeal of the Corn Laws.

We must pass in review a few more incidents in this most extraordinary five years of Parliamentary history.

"When I go down to the manufacturing districts," said Cobden in that same speech, "I know that I shall be returning to a gloomy scene. I know that starvation is stalking through the land, and that men are perishing for want of the merest necessaries of life." And he added, with gathering emphasis, "When I witness this, and recall that there is a law which especially provides for keeping our population in absolute want, I cannot help attributing murder to the legislature of this country ; and wherever I stand, whether here or out of doors, I will denounce that system of legislative murder."

"You must untax the people's bread," that was the burden and final call of the speech.

Not long after this speech Cobden's first session in Parliament came to an end, and he betook himself to the work of the League in arousing the population to a sense of the dimensions and the significance of this great political struggle.

It was about the time of the prorogation of Parliament, when Cobden and those who laboured with him were reckoning up their forces for the campaign, that the hero of the League gathered a new recruit into the ranks—a man who was destined to perform a giant's work in the cause, and to have his name linked with that of Cobden for all time as one of the greatest and most illustrious of the reformers of the nineteenth century. The new recruit was John Bright, who was only about seven years younger than Cobden. Mr. Bright has given his own account of the memorable and touching incident from which he dates the devotion of his energies to the work in which Cobden was the League's and the country's accepted leader. This is Mr. Bright's narrative. It was spoken

in 1877. He was performing that ceremony, which
has been already mentioned, of unveiling the statue of
Richard Cobden at Bradford.*   After mentioning the
origin of the Anti-Corn-Law League, Mr. Bright
said: "I will not speak of the labours of that
League. They are known to some here. Those
times by some are forgotten, and the League and its
labours have gone into the past. Happily its
results remain, and can never be destroyed. But for
seven years the discussion on that one question—
whether it was good for a man to have half a loaf or
a whole loaf—for seven years the discussion was
maintained, I will not say with doubtful result, for
the result never was doubtful, and never could be in
such a cause ; but for five years or more we devoted
ourselves without stint ; every waking hour almost
was given up to the discussion and to the movement
in connection with this question. And there is one
incident that to me is most touching in connection
with it, which I hesitate to refer to, and yet feel I can
scarcely avoid. It was in September, in the year
1841. The sufferings throughout the country were

---

* The statue was presented to the people of Bradford by Mr. G. H.
Booth, an American citizen, a partner in a Bradford firm of merchants,
on the occasion of his retiring from business and returning to his own
country. He died, unhappily, before the memorial was completed,
but his partners carried out his design. The statue was made by Mr.
Butler, and its unveiling at the Bradford Exchange was an event
rendered doubly memorable by virtue of the noble speech made by
Mr. Bright.

fearful; and you who live now, but were not of age to observe what was passing in the country then, can have no idea of the state of the country in that year. . . . At that time I was at Leamington, and, on the day that Mr. Cobden called upon me, for he happened to be there at the time on a visit to some relations, I was in the depths of grief, I might almost say of despair, for the light and sunshine of my house had been extinguished. All that was left on earth of my young wife, except the memory of a sainted life and of a too brief happiness, was lying still and cold in the chamber above us. Mr. Cobden called upon me as his friend and addressed me, as you might suppose, with words of condolence. After a time he looked up and said, 'There are thousands of houses in England at this moment where wives, mothers, and children are dying of hunger. Now,' he said, 'when the first paroxysm of your grief is past, I would advise you to come with me, and we will never rest till the Corn Law is repealed.' I accepted his invitation. I knew that the description he had given of the homes of thousands was not an ex-aggerated description. I felt in my conscience that there was a work which somebody must do, and therefore I accepted his invitation, and from that time we never ceased to labour hard on behalf of the resolution which we had made."

A few words presently followed, in that eloquent address by the side of the new statue of Cobden,

which help to make the picture of that unresting
time of the battle of the League: "We were joined,
not by scores, but by hundreds, and afterwards by
thousands, and afterwards by countless multitudes;
and afterwards famine itself, against which we had
warred, joined us; and a great Minister was con-
verted, and minorities became majorities, and finally
the barrier was entirely thrown down. And since
then, though there has been suffering, and much
suffering, in many homes in England, yet no wife
and no mother and no little child has been starved to
death as the result of a famine made by law."

There were many exciting scenes between Cobden and the defenders of the Corn Laws in the
House of Commons during this period. One of the
most remarkable was that in which Cobden, dwelling
upon the miseries of the people caused by the Corn
Laws, sought to impress upon the House the fact
that the Ministry and the Prime Minister himself,
who refused to grant the necessary legislative relief,
could not escape from the terrible responsibility
which they incurred. "I must tell the right
honourable baronet," said Cobden, "that the whole
responsibility of the lamentable and dangerous state
of the country rests with him."

Now it had happened that, at the commencement
of this session, the private secretary to the Prime
Minister was shot in Parliament Street, and died of
the wound. The assassin turned out to be a

madman; but there was an impression in some
quarters that he had mistaken the secretary for the
Premier, and that it had been his intention to shoot
Sir Robert Peel. The country was in an excited
state at the time, and the Prime Minister, on hearing
Cobden's words, rose in a state of evident agitation,
and said:

" The honourable gentleman has stated here very
emphatically, what he has more than once stated
at the conferences of the Anti-Corn-Law League,
that he holds me individually responsible for the
distress and suffering of the country—that he
holds me personally responsible. But be the consequences of these insinuations what they may,
never will I be influenced by menaces, either in
this House, or out of this House, to adopt a course
which I consider——"

A great uproar arose, the remainder of Sir
Robert's words were lost, and Cobden was howled at,
and shrieked at, and clearly accused of attempting to
create a feeling among the sufferers in the country
which might lead to the murder of the Prime
Minister. In the confusion Cobden declared: " I
did not say that I hold the right honourable gentleman personally responsible." Peel joined many
others in shouting "You did." Cobden added: " I
have said that I hold the right honourable gentleman
responsible by virtue of his office, as the whole con-
text of what I said was sufficient to explain."

But Cobden was still the leader of only a small minority, and every effort was made to turn the incident to account to injure the cause of Free Trade by the crushing of its champion. Sir Robert Peel, in a very able speech on the question before the House, took occasion to repeat his accusation against Cobden.

When he sat down Lord John Russell defended Cobden, and said that he and those who sat near him did not attach the invidious meaning to the honourable member's words. Cobden then repeated his disclaimer, saying he had used the word " individually " as the Prime Minister had used it when he said " I passed the tariff," and added, " I treat. him as the Government, as he is in the habit of treating himself." Sir Robert briefly and stiffly accepted the explanation ; but the incident aroused a great deal of heated feeling both in the House and in the country.

There were those who said that Cobden would never recover from the prejudice of the event, and that his career was over. " They shrank away from me in the cloak room of the House, as if I were a venomous serpent," he said, speaking of that time years afterwards. But the reaction soon began. Thousands of people up and down the country resented the imputations that were attempted to be cast upon the great Free Trader. Immense meetings were held in Manchester and elsewhere to express confidence in Cobden. From Manchester Sir Thomas Potter, the mayor, sent him an address signed by 31,000 of the inhabitants, declaring their "approval of his public conduct," and their "indignation at a late attempt to give a perverted and hateful meaning to his language in Parliament."

A few years later, at the very crisis of the victory of Cobden and the League in the House of Commons, it was brought to the knowledge of Sir Robert Peel that his acceptance of Cobden's explanation was not so complete as it might have been, upon which the great statesman spoke words of keen regret that such an impression should have remained behind. Cobden most cordially responded, and from that time these two men were good friends until the untimely death of Peel about four years later.

It was in the early days of 1842 that the great Free Trade Hall in Manchester, on the site of the "Battle of Peterloo," was opened on the occasion of a gigantic League meeting. Cobden had given the ground for the building, which, with the single exception of Westminster Hall, afforded the largest space within four walls of any building in the country. Here, from the date of the opening until the Repeal of the Corn Laws, were held the greatest and most enthusiastic political meetings which had ever been held in any country under a roof. At the first meeting, which was a pattern of many others, stirring speeches were made, new subscriptions to the League Fund of upwards of £42,000 were announced, and extraordinary reports were made of the progress of the agitation in the country, and of the means which were adopted to "educate the nation" in the doctrine of Free Trade.

Towards the end of 1843 the Council of the League resolved to call upon the supporters of the movement for an additional £100,000 for the expenses of the agitation, and it was not many weeks before the amount was subscribed. One of the objects was to engage Covent Garden Theatre for fifty nights, at a rent of £3,000, for the holding of monster meetings. At one of the general Manchester meetings at this time, some startling figures were quoted as to the machinery and expenditure of the agitation. During a considerable portion of the year, upwards of 300 persons had been employed in printing and making up packets of Free Trade tracts and leaflets for distribution ; 500 were employed in distributing them ; and tracts to the number of 5,000,000 had been sent to electors, and from 3,000,000 to 4,000,000 to non-electors. Altogether in the year more than 9,000,000 copies of tracts and stamped publications had been distributed in 84 counties and in 187 boroughs. Fourteen lecturers had travelled over and held meetings in 59 counties, delivering in the year 650 lectures. In this way, before the end of

1843, nearly the £50,000 had been expended which had been called for in January; and so began the next demand for £100,000. It was in November, 1844, while this £100,000 was being spent, that a remarkable article appeared in the *Times* newspaper. This great journal had been violently opposed to the League from the beginning, and the leading article of 1844 may be taken as a token of the great impression made upon the mind and feeling of the country by the movement. It has always been known as the *"great fact"* leader, from the words with which it commenced. We give a few sentences as a good reflection of the tone, character, and force of the agitation : " *The League is a great fact.* It would be foolish, nay rash, to deny its importance. It is a great fact that there should have been created in the homesteads of our manufacturers a confederacy devoted to this agitation of one political question, persevering in it year after year, shrinking from no trouble, dismayed by no danger, making light of every obstacle. It demonstrates the hardy strength of purpose and the indomitable will by which Englishmen, working together for a great object, are armed and animated. . It is a great fact that at one meeting at Manchester more than forty manufacturers should subscribe on the spot each at least £100, some £300, some £400, some £500, for the advancement of a measure which, right or wrong, just or unjust, expedient or injurious, they at least believe it to be their duty or their interest, or both, to advance in every possible way. . . *A new power has arisen in the State;* and maids and matrons flock to theatres as though it were but a new 'translation from the French.' "

Much of the spirit and substance of the article was hostile to the League and to the Repeal of the Corn Laws; but there was that in the text of it which led many to think, who had not thought so before, that Cobden's battle was in a fair way of being won.

The influence upon the public mind of the great agitation was subject to fluctuations. In 1843, and more especially in 1844, the British corn harvest was plentiful, and the price of wheat ran low, and the working and labouring population were better off. Upon this the masses of the people grew less eager on the question of Corn-law Repeal. But there was another aspect to these conditions. The farmers were in a bad way. The good harvests did not compensate them for the low prices, for they were paying rents which had been fixed when prices were much higher. So once again, as in 1814 and 1815, Parliament was called upon to consider the condition of agriculture. It was upon this subject that Cobden made a Free Trade speech in the House, in March, 1845. Its object was to prove that the distress among the farmers was the effect of the Corn Laws. It was a speech full of close practical reasoning, abounding in information about the business of farming, and it is said to have been the most effective House of Commons speech he ever made. Mr. Morley speaks thus of its effect upon Sir Robert Peel : " The Prime Minister had followed every sentence with earnest attention ; his face grew more and more solemn as the argument proceeded. At length he crumpled up the notes he had been taking, and was heard by an onlooker, who was close by, to say to Mr. Sidney Herbert, who sat next him on the bench, " *You* must answer this, for *I* cannot."

Sir Robert Peel was walking across Palace Yard that night with Sir Emerson Tenant, who remarked : " That speech of Cobden's would be hard to answer ;" to which the Prime Minister, with a certain suppressed vehemence, replied : " It is *unanswerable !* "

CHAPTER X.

THE DOWNFALL OF THE CORN LAWS.

IN the month of June in that year (1845) at a meeting in London, while the movement was still labouring under a certain degree of depression by reason of the two good harvests, Cobden said, speaking of the Ministers : " What are they thinking about as to the repeal of the Corn Laws ? I know it as well as if I were in their hearts. It is this : they

arc all agreed that this Corn Law cannot be maintained—no, not a rag of it—during a period of
scarcity prices, of a famine season, such as we had
in 1839, 1840, and 1841. They know it. They are
prepared, when such a time comes, to abolish the
Corn Law, and they have made up their minds to it.
. . . They are going to repeal it, as I told you—
mark my words—at a season of distress. That
distress may come; aye, three weeks of showery
weather when the wheat is in bloom, or ripening,
would repeal these Corn Laws. But how? We had
a taste of it in 1839, 1840, and 1841. Are the people
of this country to be subjected to another ordeal
before this Corn Law is repealed? What provision is
made against that calamity?"

These words are made remarkable by the sequence
of events. "It was," says Mr. Morley, "the wettest
autumn in the memory of man. Mr. Bright was
travelling in Scotland. The rain came over the hills
in a downpour that never ceased by night or by
day. *It was the rain that rained away the Corn
Laws.*"

In that same autumn, when men's minds were
filled with gloomy apprehensions of the consequences
of a wet harvest, came the news of a potato famine
in Ireland. The people of that country lived upon
potatoes; the plant took a blight, and the population
of Ireland stood face to face with starvation.

Then Sir Robert Peel could hold out no longer

against the conviction which had for months, and even for years, been stealing into his mind, that the Corn Laws must go. On the last day of October the Cabinet met, but Sir Robert could not persuade his colleagues to follow him in a surrender to the proposals of the Anti-Corn-Law League. Some were with him, but Lord Stanley* and the Duke of Wellington led the other side. The consultation lasted some days, but there was no decision.

In this crisis Lord John Russell, the leader of the Whig Opposition, who had never yet joined the Free Traders, published a letter addressed to his constituents of the City of London, expressing great concern that the Cabinet had made no announcement of a policy in the face of threatened calamity, and declaring for the Repeal of the Corn Laws. After explaining his desire during many years to arrive at a compromise on this question, he said, " It is no longer worth while to contend for a fixed duty. Let us then unite to put an end to a system which has been proved to be the blight of commerce, the bane of agriculture, the source of bitter divisions among classes, the cause of penury, fever, mortality, and crime among the people."

It was only in the previous June that the annual Free Trade motion of Mr. Villiers was defeated by a majority of 132. Now the two great party leaders of the House of Commons were for Repeal. But Sir

---

* The late Lord Derby.

G

Robert could not carry his colleagues with him, an
he resigned.* Lord John Russell, called upon by th
Queen, attempted to form a Ministry, but failec
through some difference of opinion among the leadei
of his party on questions other than the Corn Laws.

In the meanwhile Cobden and the League wer
arousing the country, and the popular excitemer
was without parallel in the history of the move
ment. The Executive Council of the League resolve
to make a call for subscriptions for a quarter of
million sterling; at a great League meeting i
Manchester on the 23rd of December twenty-thre
persons gave in their names for a thousand pound
each, and within an hour and a half the subscriptio
amounted to £60,000. Within a month the tota
had run up to £150,000.

On the failure of Lord John Russell to make
Government Sir Robert Peel returned to office, an
the Cabinet, with the exception of Lord Stanley (wh
left the Ministry and became for many years afte
the champion of the lost cause of Protection), con
curred with Sir Robert Peel in a measure for th
abolition of the Corn Laws in three years. Durin
those three years there was to be a sliding scale, witl
ten shillings duty when wheat was under forty-eigh
shillings a quarter, and four shillings when the pric
reached fifty-eight shillings. After that there was t
be a nominal duty of one shilling a quarter.

* December 5th, 1845.

In announcing his proposals in the House* Sir Robert began his great and memorable Free Trade speech by stating; that *on the question of the Corn Laws his opinion had undergone a complete change.* This was the crowning event alike in the life of Sir Robert Peel and in that of Richard Cobden. The "Manchester manufacturer" had made a proselyte of the great Prime Minister. Sir Robert went on to declare and to argue that all the grounds on which the Corn Law had been defended had been proved to be "wholly untenable."

The question was debated for many nights. Cobden, Bright, Villiers, and other members of the League, were of course in favour of total and immediate Repeal; but they were defeated on that point, and then gave their support to the Prime Minister's proposals, which were carried by a majority of nearly a hundred votes.

It was the work of Richard Cobden in the first Parliament in which he had a seat. That which had been pronounced impossible, impracticable, the wild dream of irresponsible theorists and enthusiasts, was brought to pass by the resolutions and the votes of the men who had scouted and derided it. Seven years of Richard Cobden and the League—five years of the Member for Stockport face to face with Peel and Melbourne and Russell—had done it. "Hurrah! Hurrah!" wrote Cobden to his wife on the 26th of

* January 19th, 1846.

June, 1846, "the Corn Bill is law, and now my work is done."

That it was *his* work there is the testimony of Sir Robert Peel himself, who had sacrificed his party to his new conviction on this great question, who was very soon beaten by a large majority on another measure, and who, in the last speech that he made before he quitted office, pointed to Richard Cobden as the conqueror. "I must say," he declared, "with reference to honourable gentlemen opposite, as I say with reference to ourselves, neither of us is the party which is justly entitled to the credit of these measures. The name," he presently added, "which ought to be and will be associated with the success of these measures is the name of the man who, acting I believe, from pure and disinterested motives, has with untiring energy, by appeals to reason, enforced their necessity with an eloquence the more to be admired because it was unaffected and unadorned— the name which ought to be associated with the success of these measures is THE NAME OF RICHARD COBDEN."

CHAPTER XI.

A NEW CAREER.

WHEN Cobden was first tempted to devote himself to the great work for which he was so eminently fitted by natural gifts and by a vast knowledge of affairs, he had built up a great business, and was a prosperous man, likely, to all appearance, to make a large fortune. But he had to pay dearly for his devotion to the public welfare. "You will probably be surprised when I tell you," he wrote at this time to a friend, "that I have shared the fate of nearly all leaders in great revolutions or great reforms, by the complete sacrifice of my private prospects in life. In a word, I was a poor man at the close of my agitation. I shall not go into details, because it would involve painful reminiscences; but suffice it to say that whilst the Duke of Richmond was taunting me with the profits of my business I was suffering the complete loss of my private fortune, and I am not now afraid to confess to you that my health of body and peace of mind have suffered more in consequence of private anxieties during the last two years than from my public labours."

This trouble was to be to a great extent removed. The nation, to whom the name of Cobden was that of a hero, knew little of the sacrifices that he had made;

but the leading supporters of the League knew it. A
National Testimonial to Mr. Cobden was proposed,
and the result was that the Free Traders of the kingdom presented their great champion with a fortune of
upwards of £75,000.

He said he would withdraw into private life, but
he could not. "I am going," he wrote, "into the
wilderness to pray for a return of the taste I once
possessed for nature and simple quiet life;" but he had
to confess, "I feel how much I have lost in winning
public fame. The rough tempest has spoilt me for
the quiet haven. I fear I shall never be able to cast
anchor again."

And here the old genius, which at eight-and-
twenty would not let him lead a private life and
make a fortune in his business, beset him once again.
At the age of forty-two, worn and jaded with work
and victory and self-sacrifice, he was impelled to say
to his friend Paulton, the brilliant Free Trade
lecturer : "It seems as if some mesmeric hand were
on my brains, or I was possessed by an unquiet
fiend urging me forward in spite of myself. On
Thursday I thought as I went to the meeting * that
I should next day be a quiet and happy man. Next
day brings me a suggestion from a private friend of
the Emperor of Russia assuring me that if instead of
going to Italy and Egypt [which he was to visit to
restore him to health] I would take a trip to St.

* The final meeting for the suspension of the League.

Petersburg, I could exercise an important influence upon the mind of Nicholas. Here I am at Llangollen, blind to the loveliness of Nature, and only eager to be on the road to Russia, taking Madrid, Vienna, Berlin, and Paris by the way! Let me see my boy to-morrow, who waits my coming at Machynlleth, and if he do not wean me I am quite gone past recovery."

He was staying in Wales, for his wife was a Welsh lady. He had married in 1840, when the League was young, and when his private business was prosperous.

The old yearning had its way with him. " I am going on a private agitating tour through the continent of Europe," he wrote presently to Mr. Henry Ashworth.

And he made something very like a triumphal journey through Europe. Among emperors, kings, statesmen, poets, historians, economists, he was the hero of the time.

He discussed politics, trade, constitutionalism, social progress, economic reform, and sound international relations among the nations, with the Pope, with Louis Philippe, Guizot, Odillon Barrot, de Tocqueville, Bastiat, Dumas, the Czar, Von Humboldt, Prince Metternich, the King of Prussia. He was fêted and feasted and made much of everywhere; and he studied great political and international questions with more than the old insight keenness and masterful comprehension.

While he was abroad a general election occurred ; he was returned at once to the House of Commons for Stockport and for the West Riding of Yorkshire, and he sat for the West Riding for the next ten years.

After his victory over the Corn Laws Cobden's career as a politician was that which was foreshadowed in his earliest political essays. He was a great master of foreign politics and the apostle of those doctrines of peace and of non-intervention in the affairs of other countries which he had propounded so clearly and so forcibly in the anonymous character of a "Manchester manufacturer." In Parliament and out of Parliament he advocated financial reform, international arbitration, direct in preference to indirect taxation, and the abolition of the Parliamentary oath. He denounced the war policy in all its forms, and opposed the maintenance of large armaments. It was the time of what was known as the "spirited foreign policy" of Lord Palmerston, and Cobden was a consistent, powerful, and eloquent opponent of that policy.

Peel's Bill for the Repeal of the Corn Laws took final effect at the end of three years on the 1st of February, 1849. On the last night in January there was a great, joyous, commemorative meeting of the League in the Free Trade Hall at Manchester. "Speeches were made and choruses were sung until midnight," says Mr. Morley; "and when twelve

o'clock sounded, the assembly broke out in loud
and long-sustained cheers to welcome the dawn of
the day which had at last brought Free Trade in
Corn."

Once it happened, however, in the succeeding
years, that the League had to be restored to life. In
1852 Lord Palmerston's Government was overthrown,
and a Tory Government was formed by Lord Derby,
the very man who (then Lord Stanley) had left Sir
Robert Peel's Cabinet when Sir Robert decided to
throw over the Corn Laws. Then the Protectionists
took heart of grace, and there was an agitation among
the landed interests· for the re-enactment of the
Corn Laws. Conservatives generally in the country
rallied round the Protectionist standard. Peel was
dead. So the old Council of the Anti-Corn-Law
League was called together ; an enthusiastic meeting was held at Manchester ; the subscription list
amounted to £70,000, and the work and organisation of the League were begun afresh. But after
the appeal to the country, Mr. Disraeli, the leader for
the Government in the House of Commons, found it
necessary to abandon the Protectionist policy, and
the reaction against Free Trade was for the time at
an end.

The long story of Cobden's career as a politician
and statesman from that time forth can only be
touched upon here in points and incidents. A bare
narrative of the part that he played, in and out of

Parliament, in political council, in public and international movements, and in his writings, would involve long explanations of such matters of history as the great revolutionary movement on the Continent of Europe in 1848 and 1849; the struggle of the States of Italy to free themselves from domestic tyranny and foreign domination; the terrible suppression of revolt in Poland and Hungary; the Chinese war; the Crimean war; the Indian mutiny; the great American War of Secession; and the Schleswig-Holstein war. In all these great questions he sought to restrain this country from interference in foreign wars and quarrels. At the same time, in a tone and spirit exhibiting a most exceptional insight into the bearings and tendencies of events and developments abroad, he advocated the adoption of measures and lines of policy calculated to bring about happy solutions as far as possible of international difficulties.

He never advocated holding aloof from foreign affairs when it should appear that good might be done by the exercise of the influence of the British Government. There is a good example in connection with the Hungarian struggle for independence when Russia helped Austria to crush the rebellion. The sympathy of the people of England was strong on the side of the Hungarians, and there was much indignation at the interference of Russia. But Lord Palmerston, the Prime Minister, who usually played an active part in all foreign questions, this time did nothing, and Cobden, while he was opposed to intervention by arms, contended that the circumstances were such that if Palmerston had simply entered a verbal protest Russia would not have invaded Hungary. Cobden and his friend Bright were the leaders of the section of Liberal politicians who were strongly opposed to the policy of our great war with Russia in the Crimea in defence of the Turkish Empire. England had not then been engaged in any great war for nearly forty years, and the war feeling in the country was so strong for awhile as to reflect a good deal of unpopularity upon the Free Trade heroes. A little later the question of the merits of a war in which we were engaged in China was very keenly discussed. By this time there is an overwhelming preponderance of judgment among politicians, historians, and others, that the Crimean war ought to have been avoided, and that the war against the Chinese was an unjust one ; but no credit in the country was to be won at that time by propounding such views. In February, 1857, in the House of Commons, Cobden proposed a motion to the effect that the violent measures of the British forces at Canton were not justified. On that motion Cobden beat the Government by a majority of sixteen, and Lord Palmerston appealed to the country.

This was the memorable general election of 1857, after we had beaten Russia, and when the old warlike ardour of the country was still rampant.

There was a vague reaction against what was called the "Manchester School" in politics—the School, as it was understood, of trade above all things, of non-intervention, and of "peace at any price." Cobden's doctrine was very different from that of "peace at any price," but popular passion is not discriminating. Cobden was a candidate for Huddersfield, and was defeated; Mr. Bright and Mr. Milner Gibson lost their seats at Manchester; and two other conspicuous supporters of the views advocated by Cobden and Bright—Mr. W. J. Fox at Oldham and Mr. Miall at Rochdale—were left out of the new Parliament.

Cobden remained in retirement from Parliamentary work for two years. It was during this time that private trouble befell him in connection with the investment of a large portion of the fortune that had been presented to him by the grateful Free Traders of England in commemoration of the Repeal of the Corn Laws. He had purchased a large number of shares in the Illinois Railway, in the United States, which seemed to be an exceedingly promising undertaking. But the property was so slow in developing into a profitable concern as to land Cobden in very great embarrassments. It is very strong evidence of the estimation in which he was held by those among whom he had laboured in the public service that there seemed to be no limit to the impulse of

generosity to help him.   In 1858 the late Mr.
Thomasson, one of his colleagues of the League, helped
him out of his difficulties for the time in a most
munificent manner.   In 1860 his affairs grew worse.
Other investments had not turned out well.   Then
the men of the Manchester School took the whole
case into consideration, and a testimonial of a much
more private character than that of 1846 was raised,
amounting to some £40,000.   Less than a hundred
men made up that sum, and he never knew their
names.   It should be noticed that when this noble
gift was made to him he had earned his second great
title to the gratitude of the wealthy trading and
manufacturing class by his splendid success in the
negotiation of the Commercial Treaty with France,
of which some account must presently be given.

By this time he was again in the House of
Commons.   While he was absent in America, partly
for the purpose of looking after his investment in
American Railways, the Government of Lord Derby
was defeated upon the Reform Bill known as the Bill
of the Fancy Franchises,"* and there was an appeal
to the country.   In that election the borough of Rochdale (the town of Mr. Bright's residence and factory)
returned Cobden to Parliament without a contest,
and in his absence.

When Cobden landed at Liverpool, once again
a Member of Parliament, he was met by an offer

* Mr. Bright's phrase.

from Lord Palmerston to make him President of the
Board of Trade with a seat in the Cabinet ; and the
offer was backed up by a letter from Lord John
Russell, pressing the office upon his acceptance, and
saying, "If you refuse I do not see a prospect of
amalgamating the Liberal Party during my lifetime.
In these circumstances I think it is a *duty* for
you to accept the office of President of the Board
of Trade."

So, just as at the end of his first five years in
Parliament—advocating the Repeal of the Corn Laws
—he broke down the opposition of the greatest leading statesman of the time—so, thirteen years later,
after fighting in the face even of popular feeling
against the war policy of the Liberal Party to which
he belonged, he found himself urged at once by
Lord Palmerston and by Lord John Russell to
take a place in the Cabinet among the advisers
of the Crown, and was told that his presence there
was essential to the formation of a Government !
And this was after a general election, only two years
later than the election in which he and Bright,
Gibson, Fox, and Miall were driven from Parliament
by five great popular constituencies !

When he arrived at Liverpool he knew nothing of
what had happened, and was not aware that he was
again a Member of Parliament. "As I came up the
Mersey," he wrote, "I little dreamed of the reception
which awaited me. Crowds of friends were ready

to greet and cheer me," and before he left the ship he opened the letters from Lord Palmerston and Lord John Russell. At the hotel more than 100 of the leading men of Liverpool presented him with an address, while a deputation from Rochdale met him at Manchester, and everybody pressed him to accept office. But he could not. "So great is the pressure put upon me," he said, "that if it were Lord Granville, or even Lord John, at the head of affairs, I should be obliged, greatly against my will, to be a Right Honourable," but to accept office under Lord Palmerston was impossible. "With my recorded opinions of Lord Palmerston's public conduct during the last dozen years," he wrote to his wife, "in which opinions I have experienced no change, were I suddenly to jump at the offer of a place under him I should ruin myself in my own self-respect, and ultimately lose the confidence of the very men who are in this moment of excitement urging me to enter his Cabinet."

He had an interview with Lord Palmerston, who sought most strongly to persuade him to accept office; but he was steadfast in his refusal.

He accepted, however, at the same moment an invitation to a reception given by Lady Palmerston at Cambridge House the next night, and giving an account of the visit, he wrote: "As I came away 'Jacob Omnium' and I were squeezed into a corner together, and he remarked, "You are the greatest political monster that ever was seen in this house. There never was before seen such a curiosity as a man who refused a Cabinet Office from Lord Palmerston and then came to visit him here."

CHAPTER XII.

THE COMMERCIAL TREATY WITH FRANCE.

IT was in 1859 and 1860 that Cobden was engaged in the second great work of his political life— the negotiation of the Commercial Treaty with the Emperor Napoleon. The scheme originated with Cobden's friend, M. Chevalier, the great French Free Trader. Much of the preliminary arrangement of the scheme was between Cobden and Mr. Gladstone, then Chancellor of the Exchequer, at Hawarden Castle. Cobden, under a commission from the Government in London, went to Paris for the purpose of persuading the Emperor and his Ministers of the wisdom of a Commercial Treaty, to encourage trade between France and England by the reduction or abolition of numerous duties on goods between the two countries. Cobden's diary gives a very interesting account of his interview at the Palace of St. Cloud with Napoleon III., in which by sheer practical argument and the marshalling of facts he talked the Emperor into favour of a policy of

Free Trade. "On my giving him a description of the reforms effected by Sir Robert Peel, and the great reverence in which his name is held," says Cobden, in the last words of his account of his conversation with the Emperor, "he said, 'I am charmed and flattered at the idea of performing a similar work in my country ; but it is very difficult in France to make Reforms—we make Revolutions in France, not Reforms.'"

Cobden had more difficulty with some of the French Ministers than with the Emperor. M. Fould, for example, brought forward "many of the old fallacies about being inundated with British goods, labourers being thrown out of work, and so forth." "I had to give him the first lesson in political economy," Cobden writes.

This great feat was accomplished by force almost alone of Cobden's wonderful ability, his mastery of the whole subject, his persuasiveness in argument, and his natural tact. He was ably assisted by Sir Louis Mallet, who, for the arrangement of the details, accompanied Cobden to Paris in an official capacity as representing the Board of Trade. The difficulties which had to be overcome in Paris were stupendous ; while in England—for Peel was dead—Cobden met with no very great or cordial help from any member of the Government except Mr. Gladstone, whose position as a distinguished statesman in the administration, and whose clear comprehension of the diffi-

H

culties that had to be encountered, alone rendered
possible the success of Cobden's exertions.

When the task was accomplished, Mr. John
Bright visited his old friend Cobden in Paris, and the
two great Anti-Corn-Law Leaguers had an interesting interview with the Emperor. In describing the
visit afterwards, Mr. Bright told how much he was
struck by the great confidence which Napoleon
seemed to feel in Cobden. At that interview the two
English visitors strongly urged upon the Emperor
to abolish the passport system between England and
France. Napoleon was much impressed by their
arguments. Cobden returned to this subject per-
sistently, for some days after that, in his communi-
cations with the French Ministers, and in less than
three weeks after the conversation between Cobden,
Bright, and Napoleon, the passport system, as far as
it affected British subjects visiting Paris, was abolished
by the French Government, and this was followed by
a cheapening of the postal arrangements between
England and France. " Thus," wrote Cobden to his
friend Bright, " in the same year we have the tariff
[the treaty], abolition of passports, and a new postal
facility. Why should not our Foreign Office accomplish some good of this kind ?"

There was some talk of the Government pro-
posing to make a vote of money to Cobden in
recognition of his great services in the negotiation
of this treaty ; but, whether or not there was any

such intention on the part of the Government, Cobden let Mr. Bright and his friends know that he would not have accepted such a vote. A little later Lord Palmerston made known to Cobden the Queen's desire that he should be offered a baronetcy, or be made a Privy Councillor, which Cobden said he could not accept, adding, "The only reward I desire is to live to witness an improvement in the relations of the two great neighbouring nations which have been brought into more intimate connection by the Treaty of Commerce."

, The result of the treaty was a quickly expanding and quite enormous increase in the trade between France and England, to the very great advantage and profit of both countries. Another consequence was the gradual subsidence of the jealousy and un-friendly feeling between the two countries which had been a source of so much unnecessary expenditure and so much danger of a rupture. It was incidental to the Commercial Treaty negotiations that a dis-tinguished French statesman, M. Drouyn de Lhuys, spoke of Cobden as "the international man," a designation which has been very largely quoted.

When the treaty was submitted to Parliament, Mr. Gladstone spoke in these eloquent words of the great feat which Cobden had accomplished: "Rare is the privilege of any man who having fourteen years ago rendered to his country one signal and splendid service, now again, within the same brief space of life decorated neither by rank nor title, bearing no mark to distinguish him from the people whom he serves, has been permitted again to perform a great and memorable service to his country."

Of this treaty Mr. Bright has spoken thus : " I venture to say that there is no act of any statesman's life that may be looked back to with more unalloyed pleasure by him who did it, or by his friends who stood by him and commended it, than that great act of the Commercial Treaty with our neighbouring country, France."

In commemoration of their many interviews, and of the work of the Commercial Treaty, the Emperor Napoleon sent Cobden, as a present, a handsome vase from the palace of St. Cloud, which is now to be seen at the South Kensington Museum, Mrs. Cobden having presented it to the nation after her husband's death.

It was some six or seven months after the ratification of the Commercial Treaty that Cobden, coming home from a sojourn in Egypt and Syria, had his last interview with the Emperor Napoleon at the Palace of the Tuileries. The substance of his conversation with the Emperor forms a brief exposition of his views on the great Eastern question, which now, as then, is frequently under more or less serious discussion. He suggested that England, France, Austria, and Russia should bind each other and themselves to an agreement not to take one inch of Turkish territory ; that it should also be agreed not to help Turkey in any of her troubles ; that the Christians of those regions should be permitted to drive back the Turks into Asia ; that the Greeks should be allowed to possess themselves of their ancient capital of Constantinople. Among the facts which he urged on the question were, that the Christians in Turkey were the only element of progress, possessing all the wealth, carrying on all the commerce, the arts, and the professions ; that the Turks did not possess a single vessel engaged in the foreign trade ; and that all the commerce of the Black Sea and of the eastern ports of the Mediterranean were falling naturally into the hands of the Greeks.

In the great American War of Secession, Cobden was on the side of the North. Early in 1865, when Lincoln had been murdered, and a spirit of vengeance was abroad in the North, and General Lee's life was in danger, a letter from Cobden, urging forgiveness and conciliation towards the South, was shown by the late Mr. J. W. Garratt to President Johnson, who, on reading it, burst into tears, saying : " Cobden is right : there must be conciliation, not vengeance."

Cobden advocated large changes in the rules of blockades and in the regulations affecting the safety of mercantile ships in time of war. Indeed, he was until the day of his death in the midst of public affairs, always engaged in the advocacy of practical reforms and of measures for the benefit not of his own country only but of the human race.

CHAPTER XIII

LAST DAYS.

APART from his actual engagement in public movements and public affairs, Cobden's life does not afford
many incidents or episodes for the biographer.

The most terrible grief of his life was the loss of
his only son, in 1856, a very promising youth, fifteen
years of age, who died of scarlet fever at his school in
Heidelberg. By both parents the child was idolised,
and the grief of the mother and the father is one of
the most painful stories of the kind in modern
biography. All their personal friends agree that the
father was never the same man again after this blow,
and the shock to the mother was such that, though
she lived afterwards for more than twenty years, it was
impossible for those with whom she lived ever to for-
get the effect upon her of that news from Heidelberg.

His natural vigour of mind and intense interest in
public affairs helped Cobden after awhile in some
degree to recover tone and spirit; but he was a
man of keen and tender social and domestic feeling,
never so happy as in his home with his children. He
had not only a great love for children, but was full of
a peculiar thoughtfulness and consideration for them.
Of this his friend, Mr. Thomas Bayley Potter, relates a
touching incident. Only a few hours before setting out

for Paris from Newhaven, to enter upon the hard work
of the Commercial Treaty, Cobden was with Mr. Potter and members of his family at Devil's Dyke, near
Brighton. One of Mr. Potter's sons, a child about
eight years of age, was much pleased with a new
india-rubber ball, and Cobden joined the child in
throwing and catching the ball on the grassy slope.
At length Cobden threw the ball a little too far, and
it ran down the steep declivity out of reach of recovery. The flash of disappointment on the child's face
so affected Cobden that he was about to attempt the
perilous descent to recover the plaything, when Mr.
Potter grasped his arm, and laughed, and said, " No,
we cannot afford to risk the safety of our great tribune
of the people for a wretched ball." Cobden's mind,
as may be supposed, was sufficiently occupied with
letters and interviews and grave affairs of state in
these last few hours before starting for Paris ; but the
pressure of affairs did not prevent him from sending
to the little boy next morning a parcel containing a
handsome new india-rubber ball, and a pretty little
letter in simple words for the child's own reading.

Cobden's last speech in Parliament was one in
which he contended that the Government should not
be allowed to manufacture for itself any article which
could be obtained from private producers in a com-
petitive market. His last speech in life was addressed
to his constituents in Rochdale, in November, 1864.
This was the speech in which he said : " If I were five-

and-twenty or thirty, instead of being unhappily twice
that number of years, I would take Adam Smith in
hand; I would not go beyond him, I would have no
politics in it : I would take Adam Smith in hand, and
I would have a League for Free Trade in Land just as
we had a League for Free Trade in Corn."

The last letter Cobden ever wrote was addressed
to Mr. Thomas Bayley Potter, on the 22nd of March,
1865. Mr. Potter had sent him a letter from Mr. J.
Stuart Mill, suggesting schemes for the representation of minorities in elections. Cobden gave his
reasons for differing from Mr. Mill, and expressed
his preference for the division of constituencies into
sections, each section to be represented by one
member; a plan which has been to a large extent
adopted in the Reform Bill of 1885. This last letter
from Cobden was never posted. It was given to Mr.
Potter by Mrs. Cobden after her husband's death.

He was not in good health or spirits when he went
to Rochdale ; and he was much exhausted after that
last speech. During his illness Mr. Gladstone offered
him the honourable official post of Chairman of the
Board of Audit, at a salary of £2,000 a year, which
Cobden did not accept. He suffered much during the
winter with attacks of asthma. On the 21st of March
he travelled to London to take part in a discussion
on the Canadian fortifications, and took lodgings in
Suffolk Street. His zeal on the subject of the defence
of Canada was such that he made the journey contrary

to the advice of his friends. But he did not attend the discussion. He took cold at the station in the bitter east wind, the cold developed into an attack of his old enemy bronchitis ; and he never left the house again. On Sunday morning, April 1st, 1865, Mr. Bright was with him at his bedside, and saw him die.

" He was buried," says Mr. Morley, " by the side of his son in the little churchyard at Lavington, on the slope of the hill among the pine woods."

It was thirty-three years since, as an obscure young Manchester cotton printer, he had written to his brother of the mysterious yearning in his heart for some great work to be done in the world. In that thirty-three years he had done a work the like of which he could not have dreamed of when he gave that expression to his feeling. He had become known to all nations as a great and good man, who did more to lift politics out of the wrong groove, and to give the art of Government a better direction from his day forth, than any other man in his time.

On the day after Cobden's death, Mr. Disraeli said : " There are some members of Parliament who, though they may not be present, are still members of this House, are independent of dissolutions, of the caprices of constituencies, and even of the course of time. I think that Mr. Cobden was one of these men."*

* To Mr. T. B. Potter some years later Mr. Disraeli wrote : " We do not in Parliament miss merely Cobden's wisdom in council, but the sweetness and amiability of his disposition."

Mr. Bright felt the loss of his friend too deeply to be able to say more than a few broken words in the House of Commons that day. " The time," he said, "which has elapsed since, in my presence, the manliest and gentlest spirit that ever quitted or tenanted a human form took its flight is so short that I dare not even attempt to give utterance to the feelings by which I am oppressed. . . I have only to say that after twenty years of most intimate and almost brotherly friendship, I little knew how much I loved him until I had lost him."

" There is not a homestead in the country," said Mr. Bright a dozen years later, standing by the side of Cobden's statue at Bradford, " in which there is not added comfort from his labours, not a cottage, the dwellers in which have not steadier employment, higher wages, and a more solid independence. . . . And let this be said of him for generations to come, as long as the great men of England are spoken of in the English language—let it be said of him that Richard Cobden gave the labours of a life that he might confer upon his countrymen perfect freedom of industry, and with it not that blessing only, but its attendant blessings of plenty and peace."

Close upon twenty years after Cobden's death, in the autumn of 1884, Mr. Gladstone, among a party of gentlemen in a country house in Scotland, in the course of a casual conversation on great men and the reverence due to them, said : " Take one example.

There is Cobden. I do not know that there is in any period a man whose public career and life were nobler or more admirable than Cobden's."

Some few months later, in [December, 1884, while Mr. Gladstone's mind was, perhaps, not wholly free from perplexity as to the right path of policy for an English statesman in the difficult business of the war in the Soudan, the Premier, writing to Mr. Thomas Bayley Potter on a question of the work of the Cobden Club, said, " I never thought more highly than now of the admirable man whose fame you have done so much to uphold."

CHAPTER XIV.

THE COBDEN CLUB.

WITHIN a year after the death of Mr. Cobden, a few of the friends whom he had left behind him were talking of the work that he did, the example that he set, the political principles which he had caused to be applied to practical politics, and the political education which the Anti-Corn-Law League, then long since dissolved, had spread abroad in the land, and between Mr. Bright and Mr. Thorold Rogers the suggestion arose that a Cobden Club should be founded, to keep green the memory of the " Apostle of Free Trade," to do something, if the need should

arise, to prevent the country from falling back from
the economic principles which Cobden had brought
into such substantial practical recognition, and to
work for the extension to foreign countries of the
Free Trade doctrines of Cobden, of Peel, and of
Gladstone. And between Mr. Bright and Mr.
Thorold Rogers it was agreed that Mr. Thomas
Bayley Potter should be requested to undertake the
task of founding the Club, of organising it, and of
presiding over its work. For Mr. Potter, who had
long been a very intimate personal and political
friend of Cobden's, had been accepted as Cobden's
successor in the representation of Rochdale in Parliament; and he had distinguished himself, during
the last few years of Cobden's career, as President
of the Union and Emancipation Society which, on
the lines of the Anti-Corn-Law League, had nobly
laboured, during the American War of Secession, to
keep popular feeling in this country true to the
interests of the Northern States of America in that
great civil war, and faithful to the great cause of
slave emancipation in America and popular government all over the world.

The suggestion was adopted. Mr. Potter had in
his young days seen much of the working of the
League, of which his father, Sir Thomas Potter, the
first Mayor of Manchester, was one of the earliest
members; and he had learned valuable experience in
the working of the Union and Emancipation Society,

and in other public organisations for progress at that time. He founded the Cobden Club, and made it a great success from the beginning. Cobden had been described by a French Statesman as "the international man," and Mr. Potter took measures to secure that this should be an international club. It is indeed the only great international political association in existence. It has members in both hemispheres and in almost every civilised country, and its famous motto, "Free Trade, Peace, Good-will among Nations," which was suggested by Mr. Goldwin Smith, is known wherever the English language is understood.

The specific object for which the Club was established was that of "encouraging the growth and diffusion of those economical and political principles with which Mr. Cobden's name is associated." Mr. Gladstone presided at the first banquet of the Club, and made a most eloquent speech on Mr. Cobden's life, character, and work, and on the political principles to which his energies were devoted. In succeeding years the chairmen of these banquets have been Lord Houghton, Earl Russell, Mr. Villiers, the Duke of Argyll, Mr. Gladstone again, Earl Granville, Mr. Milner Gibson, Mr. W. E. Baxter, M. Michel Chevalier, the Marquis of Hartington, Mr. W. E. Forster, the Earl of Northbrook, the Earl Spencer, the Earl of Derby, Mr. Joseph Chamberlain, Lord Carlingford, and Sir Charles Dilke. It was stated in Mr. Potter's speech at the annual meeting of the Club in

1880, that of the fourteen statesmen constituting **Mr.**
Gladstone's Cabinet twelve were members of the
Cobden Club, and when the Gladstone Ministry
resigned in June, 1885, thirteen of the sixteen Cabinet
Ministers had their names on the Club roll.

The speeches made from the chair at the Cobden
Club banquets form an interesting and valuable
contribution to the library of Cobdenic literature.
In the years since the foundation of the Club more
than a million and half of Cobdenic books and publications have been distributed at home and abroad ;
and during 1885, to counteract what is called the
" Fair Trade " movement (a new form of agitation for
the taxation of imports), and to educate the new
electors in Free Trade principles, many millions of
leaflets on Free Trade and other Cobdenic subjects
have been circulated.

It is some token of the international interest in
Cobden's name and work that, in these few years since
the great Free Trader's death, there have been enrolled
among the honorary members of the Club the names
of such men as President Garfield, M. Léon Gambetta,
Nubar Pasha, Prince Hassan, General Garibaldi, the
Rev. Henry Ward Beecher, Mr. John Bigelow, Mr.
Cyrus Field, Mr. Ralph Waldo Emerson, Mr. William
Lloyd Garrison, M. Emile de Laveleye, Mr. Henry
Wadsworth Longfellow, the Vicomte Ferdinand de
Lesseps, H. I. H. Prince Jerome Napoleon, M. Emile
Ollivier, H. R. H. the Comte de Paris, M. Rouher,

M. Léon Say, the Hon. David A. Wells, and other great leaders in thought and action, in politics and statesmanship, in the two hemispheres.

The work of the "World's Workers" goes on long after they have left us. Richard Cobden's achievements were great, and even astounding, seeing how new were the ideas and the elements which he introduced into the field of practical politics and statesmanship, and how short was the time given to him in which to labour. But what he accomplished was only the beginning of the splendid enterprise to which his days were devoted. The world had almost slept for two or three generations upon the economic discoveries of Adam Smith, until the "Wealth of Nations" fell into the hands of Richard Cobden; and even the magnificent demonstration of the soundness of the Free Trade doctrine which was given to the world in the conversion of Sir Robert Peel by the "Manchester manufacturer"—and in the Repeal of the Corn Laws and its marvellous results—is not enough, in two or three generations, to remove the mountains of prejudice, of fallacy, and of vested interests in monopoly which stand in the way. Cobden the Worker in the nineteenth century, like Adam Smith the Thinker in the eighteenth, found commerce struggling on against old-world delusions while the relations between nation and nation were very much what we find the relations to be between the

tribes and potentates of Central Africa. Political
Economy may be said to have begun with Adam
Smith; there is a sense in which Modern History
may be said to have begun with Richard Cobden.
Ever since the revival of learning and the discovery
of America men have been found proudly declaring
that the world has passed over the line of mediæval
into modern history: but there will be great historians
—students of the phenomena of the modern spirit in
domestic and international politics—who will rise
up, by-and-by, to tell the world that the real commencement of modern history was when the foremost
of the principalities and states of the world began to
work out the principle of "Free Trade, Peace, Good-
will among Nations."

*(Our Portrait is from a Print published by Dickinsons, New Bond Street
London).*

Illustrated, Fine-Art, and other Volumes.

Art, The Magazine of. Yearly Volume. With 500 choice Engravings. 16s.

After London; or, Wild England. By RICHARD JEFFERIES. 10s. 6d.

Bismarck, Prince. By CHARLES LOWE, M.A. Two Vols., demy 8vo. With two Portraits. 24s.

Bright, John, Life and Times of. By W. ROBERTSON. 7s. 6d.

British Ballads. With 275 Original Illustrations. Two Vols. Cloth, 7s. 6d. each.

British Battles on Land and Sea. By JAMES GRANT. With about 600 Illustrations. Three Vols., 4to, £1 7s.; Library Edition, £1 10s.

British Battles, Recent. Illustrated. 4to, 9s.; Library Edition, 10s.

Butterflies and Moths, European. By W. F. KIRBY. With 61 Coloured Plates. Demy 4to, 35s.

Canaries and Cage-Birds, The Illustrated Book of. By W. A. BLAKSTON, W. SWAYSLAND, and A. F. WIENER. With 56 Fac-simile Coloured Plates, 35s. Half-morocco, £2 5s.

Cassell's Family Magazine. Yearly Vol. Illustrated. 9s.

Cathedral Churches of England and Wales. With 150 Illustrations. 21s. *Édition de luxe*, £2 2s.

Changing Year, The. With Illustrations. 7s. 6d.

Choice Dishes at Small Cost. By A. G. PAYNE. 3s. 6d.

Choice Poems by H. W. Longfellow. Illustrated. 6s.

Cities of the World: their Origin, Progress, and Present Aspect. Three Vols. Illustrated. 7s. 6d. each.

Clinical Manuals for Practitioners and Students of Medicine. A List of Volumes forwarded post free on application to the Publishers.

Colonies and India, Our, How we Got Them, and Why we Keep Them. By Prof. C. RANSOME. 1s.

Columbus, Christopher, The Life and Voyages of. By WASHINGTON IRVING. Three Vols. 7s. 6d.

Cookery, Cassell's Dictionary of. Containing about Nine Thousand Recipes, 7s. 6d.; half-roan, 9s.; Roxburgh, 10s. 6d.

Co-operators, Working Men: What they have Done, and What they are Doing. By A. H. DYKE-ACLAND and B. JONES. 1s.

Cookery, A Year's. By PHYLLIS BROWNE. Cloth gilt, or oiled cloth, 3s. 6d.

Countries of the World, The. By ROBERT BROWN, M.A., Ph.D., &c. Complete in Six Vols., with about 750 Illustrations. 4to, 7s. 6d. each.

Cromwell, Oliver: The Man and his Mission. By J. ALLANSON PICTON, M.P. Cloth, 7s. 6d.; morocco, cloth sides, 9s.

Cyclopædia, Cassell's Concise. With 12,000 subjects, brought down to the latest date. With about 600 Illustrations, 15s.; Roxburgh, 18s.

Dairy Farming. By Prof. J. P. SHELDON. With 25 Fac-simile Coloured Plates, and numerous Wood Engravings. Cloth, 31s. 6d.; half-morocco, 42s.

Decisive Events in History. By THOMAS ARCHER. With Sixteen Illustrations. Boards, 3s. 6d.; cloth, 5s.

Decorative Design, Principles of. By CHRISTOPHER DRESSER, Ph.D. Illustrated. 5s.

Deserted Village Series, The. Consisting of *Éditions de luxe* of the most favourite poems of Standard Authors. Illustrated. 2s. 6d. each.

GOLDSMITH'S DESERTED VILLAGE.	WORDSWORTH'S ODE ON IMMOR-
MILTON'S L'ALLEGRO AND IL	TALITY, AND LINES ON TIN-
PENSEROSO.	TERN ABBEY.

Dickens, Character Sketches from. SECOND and THIRD SERIES. With Six Original Drawings in each, by FREDERICK BARNARD. In Portfolio, 21s. each.

Diary of Two Parliaments. The Disraeli Parliament. By H. W. LUCY. 12s.

Dog, The By IDSTONE. Illustrated. 2s. 6d.

Dog, Illustrated Book of the. By VERO SHAW, B.A. With 28 Coloured Plates. Cloth bevelled, 35s. ; half-morocco, 45s.

Domestic Dictionary, The. An Encyclopædia for the Household. Cloth, 7s. 6d.

Doré's Adventures of Munchausen. Illustrated by GUSTAVE DORÉ. 5s.

Doré's Dante's Inferno. Illustrated by GUSTAVE DORÉ. *Popular Edition*, 21s.

Doré's Don Quixote. With about 400 Illustrations by DORÉ. 15s.

Doré's Fairy Tales Told Again. With 24 Full-page Engravings by GUSTAVE DORÉ. 5s.

Doré Gallery, The. *Popular Edition* With 250 Illustrations by GUSTAVE DORÉ. 4to, 42s.

Doré's Milton's Paradise Lost. With Full-page Drawings by GUSTAVE DORÉ. 4to, 21s.

Edinburgh, Old and New, Cassell's. Three Vols. With 600 Illustrations. 9s. each.

Educational Year-Book, The. 6s.

Egypt : Descriptive, Historical, and Picturesque. By Prof. G. EBERS. Translated by CLARA BELL, with Notes by SAMUEL BIRCH, LL.D., &c. Two Vols. With 800 Original Engravings. Vol. I., £2 5s. ; Vol. II., £2 12s. 6d. Complete in box, £4 17s. 6d.

Electrician's Pocket-Book, The. By GORDON WIGAN, M.A. 5s.

Encyclopædic Dictionary, The. A New and Original Work of Reference to all the Words in the English Language. Nine Divisional Vols. now ready, 10s. 6d. each ; or the Double Divisional Vols., half-morocco, 21s. each.

Energy in Nature. By WM. LANT CARPENTER, B.A., B.Sc. 80 Illustrations. 3s. 6d.

England, Cassell's Illustrated History of. With 2,000 Illustrations. Ten Vols. 4to, 9s. each.

English History, The Dictionary of. Cloth, 21s. ; Roxburgh, 25s.

English Literature, Library of. By Prof. HENRY MORLEY.

    VOL. I.—SHORTER ENGLISH POEMS, 12s. 6d.
    VOL. II.—ILLUSTRATIONS OF ENGLISH RELIGION, 11s. 6d.
    VOL. III.—ENGLISH PLAYS, 11s. 6d.
    VOL. IV.—SHORTER WORKS IN ENGLISH PROSE, 11s. 6d.
    VOL. V.—SKETCHES OF LONGER WORKS IN ENGLISH VERSE AND PROSE, 11s. 6d.
    Five Volumes handsomely bound in half-morocco, £5 5s.
Volumes I., II., and III. of the Popular Edition are now ready, price 7s. 6d. each.

English Literature, The Story of. By ANNA BUCKLAND. 5s.

English Literature, Dictionary of. By W. DAVENPORT ADAMS. *Cheap Edition*, 7s. 6d. ; Roxburgh, 10s. 6d.

English Poetesses. By ERIC S. ROBERTSON, M.A. 5s.

Æsop's Fables. With about 150 Illustrations by E. GRISET. Cloth, 7s. 6d.; gilt edges, 10s. 6d.

Etiquette of Good Society. 1s. ; cloth, 1s. 6d.

Family Physician, The. By Eminent PHYSICIANS and SURGEONS. Cloth, 21s. ; half-morocco, 25s.

Far, Far West, Life and Labour in the. By W. HENRY BARNEBY. With Map of Route. Cloth, 16s.

Fenn, G. Manville, Works by. *Popular Editions.* Cloth boards, 2s. each.

SWEET MACE.	THE VICAR'S PEOPLE.
DUTCH, THE DIVER ; OR, A MAN'S MISTAKE.	COBWEB'S FATHER, AND OTHER STORIES.
MY PATIENTS. Being the Notes of a Navy Surgeon.	THE PARSON O' DUMFORD. POVERTY CORNER.

Ferns, European. By JAMES BRITTEN, F.L.S. With 30 Fac-simile Coloured Plates by D. BLAIR, F.L.S. 21s.

Festival Tales. By J. F. WALLER. 3s. 6d.

Field Naturalist's Handbook, The. By the Rev. J. G. WOOD and THEODORE WOOD. 5s.

Figuier's Popular Scientific Works. With Several Hundred Illustrations in each. 3s. 6d. each.; half-calf, 6s. each.

THE HUMAN RACE.	THE OCEAN WORLD.
WORLD BEFORE THE DELUGE.	THE VEGETABLE WORLD.
REPTILES AND BIRDS.	THE INSECT WORLD.
MAMMALIA.	

Fine-Art Library, The. Edited by JOHN SPARKES, Principal of the South Kensington Art Schools. Each Book contains about 100 Illustrations. 5s. each.

TAPESTRY. By Eugene Müntz. Translated by Miss L. J. Davis.	GREEK ARCHÆOLOGY. By Maxime Collignon. Translated by Dr. J. H. Wright, Associate Professor of Greek in Dartmouth Coll., U.S.A.
ENGRAVING. By Lé Vicomte Henri Delaborde. Translated by R. A. M. Stevenson.	
THE ENGLISH SCHOOL OF PAINTING. By E. Chesneau. Translated by L. N. Etherington. With an Introduction by Prof. Ruskin.	ARTISTIC ANATOMY. By Prof. Duval. Translated by F. E. Fenton.
THE FLEMISH SCHOOL OF PAINTING. By A. J. Wauters. Translated by Mrs. Henry Rossel.	THE DUTCH SCHOOL OF PAINTING. By Henry Havard. Translated by G. Powell.

Fisheries of the World, The. Illustrated. 4to. 9s.

Five Pound Note, The, and other Stories. By G. S. JEALOUS. 1s.

Forging of the Anchor, The. A Poem. By Sir SAMUEL FERGUSON, LL.D With 20 Original Illustrations. Gilt edges, 5s.

Fossil Reptiles, A History of British. By Sir RICHARD OWEN, K.C.B., F.R.S., &c. With 268 Plates. In Four Vols., £12 12s.

Four Years of Irish History (1845-49). By Sir GAVAN DUFFY, K.C.M.G. 21s.

Franco-German War, Cassell's History of the. Two Vols. With 500 Illustrations. 9s. each.

Garden Flowers, Familiar. FIRST, SECOND, THIRD, and FOURTH SERIES. By SHIRLEY HIBBERD. With Original Paintings by F. E. HULME, F.L.S. With 40 Full-page Coloured Plates in each. Cloth gilt, in cardboard box (or in morocco, cloth sides), 12s. 6d. each.

Gardening, Cassell's Popular. Illustrated. Vols. I., II., and III., 5s. each.

Gladstone, Life of W. E. By BARNETT SMITH. With Portrait, 3s. 6d. *Jubilee Edition*, 1s.

Gleanings from Popular Authors. Two Vols. With Original Illustrations. 4to, 9s. each. Two Vols. in One, 15s.

Great Industries of Great Britain. Three Vols. With about 400 Illustrations. 4to., cloth, 7s. 6d. each.

Great Painters of Christendom, The, from Cimabue to Wilkie. By JOHN FORBES-ROBERTSON. Illustrated throughout. 12s. 6d.

Great Western Railway, The Official Illustrated Guide to the. With Illustrations, 1s. ; cloth, 2s.

Gulliver's Travels. With 88 Engravings by MORTEN. *Cheap Edition*, 5s.

Guide to Employment in the Civil Service. 3s. 6d.

Guide to Female Employment in Government Offices. 1s.

Gun and its Development, The. By W. W. GREENER. With 500 Illustrations. 10s. 6d.

Health, The Book of. By Eminent Physicians and Surgeons. Cloth, 21s. Half-morocco, 25s.

Heavens, The Story of the. By ROBERT STAWELL BALL, LL.D., F.R.S., F.R.A.S., Royal Astronomer of Ireland. With 16 *Separate Plates* printed by Chromo-Lithography, and 90 Wood Engravings. Demy 8vo, 544 pages, cloth. 31s. 6d.

Heroes of Britain in Peace and War. In Two Vols., with 300 Original Illustrations. Cloth, 5s. each.

Horse, The Book of the. By SAMUEL SIDNEY. With 25 *fac-simile* Coloured Plates. Demy 4to, 31s. 6d. ; half-morocco, £2 2s.

Horses, The Simple Ailments of. By W. F. Illustrated. 5s.

Household Guide, Cassell's. With Illustrations and Coloured Plates. Two Double Vols., half-calf, 31s. 6d.; Library Edition, Two Vols., 24s.

How to Get on. With 1,000 Precepts for Practice. 3s. 6d.

How Women may Earn a Living. By MERCY GROGAN, 1s.

India, The Coming Struggle for. By Prof. ARMINIUS VAMBÉRY. With Map in Colours. 5s.

India, Cassell's History of. By JAMES GRANT. With about 400 Illustrations. Two Vols., 9s. each.

India; the Land and the People. By Sir JAMES CAIRD, K.C.B. 10s. 6d.

In-door Amusements, Card Games, and Fireside Fun, Cassell's Book of. Illustrated. 3s. 6d.

International Portrait Gallery, The. Two Vols., each containing 20 Portraits in Colours. 12s. 6d. each.

Invisible Life, Vignettes from. By JOHN BADCOCK, F.R.M.S. Illustrated. 3s. 6d.

Italy. By J. W. PROBYN. 7s. 6d.

Kennel Guide, Practical. By Dr. GORDON STABLES. Illustrated. 2s. 6d

Khiva, A Ride to. By the late Col. FRED BURNABY. 1s. 6d.

Ladies' Physician, The. By a London Physician. 6s.

Selections from Cassell & Company's Publications.

Land Question, The. By. Prof. J. ELLIOT, M.R.A.C. 10s. 6d.

Landscape Painting in Oils, A Course of Lessons in. By A. F. GRACE. With Nine Reproductions in Colour. *Cheap Edition,* 25s.

Law, About Going to. By A. J. WILLIAMS. 2s. 6d.

London & North-Western Railway Official Illustrated Guide. 1s. ; cloth, 2s.

London, Greater. By EDWARD WALFORD. Two Vols. With about 400 Illustrations. 9s. each.

London, Old and New. Six Vols., each containing about 200 Illustrations and Maps. Cloth, 9s. each.

London's Roll of Fame. With Portraits and Illustrations. 12s. 6d.

Longfellow's Poetical Works. Illustrated. £3 3s.

Love's Extremes, At. By MAURICE THOMPSON. 5s.

Mechanics, The Practical Dictionary of. Containing 15,000 Drawings. Four Vols. 21s. each.

Medicine, Manuals for Students of. *A List forwarded post free on application.*

Microscope, The; and some of the Wonders it Reveals. 1s.

Midland Railway, Official Illustrated Guide to the. 1s. ; cloth, 2s.

Modern Artists, Some. With highly-finished Engravings. 12s. 6d.

Modern Europe, A History of. By C. A. FYFFE, M.A. Vol. I. from 1792 to 1814. 12s.

National Portrait Gallery, The. Each Volume containing 20 Portraits, printed in Chromo-Lithography. Four Vols., 12s. 6d. each ; or in Two Double Vols., 21s. each.

Natural History, Cassell's Concise. By E. PERCEVAL WRIGHT, M.A., M.D., F.L.S. With several Hundred Illustrations. 7s. 6d.

Natural History, Cassell's New. Edited by Prof. P. MARTIN DUNCAN, M.B., F.R.S., F.G.S. With Contributions by Eminent Scientific Writers. Complete in Six Vols. With about 2,000 high-class Illustrations. Extra crown 4to, cloth, 9s. each.

Natural History, Cassell's Popular. With about 2,000 Engravings and Coloured Plates. Complete in Four Vols. Cloth gilt, 42s.

Nature, Short Studies from. Illustrated. 5s.

Novels, Cassell's Shilling. Consisting of New and Original Works of Romance and Adventure by Leading Writers. Price 1s. each.

AS IT WAS WRITTEN. By S. Luska. | THE CRIMSON STAIN. By A. Bradshaw.

MORGAN'S HORROR. By G. Manville Fenn.

Nursing for the Home and for the Hospital, A Handbook of. By CATHERINE J. WOOD. *Cheap Edition.* 1s. 6d. ; cloth, 2s.

On the Equator. By H. DE W. Illustrated with Photos. 3s. 6d.

Our Homes, and How to Make them Healthy. By Eminent Authorities. Illustrated. 15s. ; half-morocco, 21s.

Our Own Country. Six Vols. With 1,200 Illustrations. Cloth, 7s. 6d. each.

Outdoor Sports and Indoor Amusements. With nearly 1,000 Illustrations. 9s.

Paris, Cassell's Illustrated Guide to. 1s. ; cloth, 2s.

Parliaments, A Diary of Two. By H. W. LUCY. The Disraeli Parliament, 1874—1880. 12s.

Paxton's Flower Garden. By Sir JOSEPH PAXTON and Prof. LINDLEY. Revised by THOMAS BAINES, F.R.H.S. Three Vols. With 100 Coloured Plates. £1 1s. each.

Peoples of the World, The. Vols. I. to V. By Dr. ROBERT BROWN. With Illustrations. 7s. 6d. each.

Perak and the Malays. By Major FRED McNAIR. Illustrated. 10s. 6d.

Photography for Amateurs. By T. C. HEPWORTH. Illustrated. 1s.; or cloth, 1s. 6d.

Phrase and Fable, Dictionary of. By the Rev. Dr. BREWER. *Cheap Edition, Enlarged*, cloth, 3s. 6d. ; or with leather back, 4s. 6d.

Pictures from English Literature. With Full-page Illustrations. 5s.

Pictures of Bird Life in Pen and Pencil. Illustrated. 21s.

Picturesque America. Complete in Four Vols., with 48 Exquisite Steel Plates and about 800 Original Wood Engravings. £2 2s. each.

Picturesque Canada. With about 600 Original Illustrations. Two Vols. £3 3s. each.

Picturesque Europe. Complete in Five Vols. Each containing 13 Exquisite Steel Plates, from Original Drawings, and nearly 200 Original Illustrations. £10 10s. ; half-morocco, £15 15s. ; morocco gilt, £26 5s. The POPULAR EDITION is published in Five Vols., 18s. each., of which Four Vols. are now ready.

Pigeon Keeper, The Practical. By LEWIS WRIGHT. Illustrated. 3s. 6d.

Pigeons, The Book of. By ROBERT FULTON. Edited and Arranged by LEWIS WRIGHT. With 50 Coloured Plates and numerous Wood Engravings. 31s. 6d. ; half-morocco, £2 2s.

Poems and Pictures. With numerous Illustrations. 5s.

Poets, Cassell's Miniature Library of the :—

BURNS. Two Vols. 2s. 6d.	MILTON. Two Vols. 2s. 6d.
BYRON. Two Vols. 2s. 6d.	SCOTT. Two Vols. 2s. 6d. [2s. 6d.
HOOD. Two Vols. 2s. 6d.	SHERIDAN and GOLDSMITH. 2 Vols.
LONGFELLOW. Two Vols. 2s. 6d.	WORDSWORTH. Two Vols. 2s. 6d.

SHAKESPEARE. Twelve Vols., in box, 15s.

Police Code, and Manual of the Criminal Law. By C. E. HOWARD VINCENT. 2s.

Popular Library, Cassell's. A Series of New and Original Works. Cloth, 1s. each.

THE RUSSIAN EMPIRE.	THE STORY OF THE ENGLISH
THE RELIGIOUS REVOLUTION	JACOBINS.
IN THE 16TH CENTURY.	DOMESTIC FOLK LORE.
ENGLISH JOURNALISM.	THE REV. ROWLAND HILL:
THE WIT AND WISDOM OF	Preacher and Wit.
THE BENCH AND BAR.	BOSWELL AND JOHNSON:
THE ENGLAND OF SHAKE-	their Companions and Con-
SPEARE.	temporaries.
THE HUGUENOTS.	THE SCOTTISH COVE-
OUR COLONIAL EMPIRE.	NANTERS.
JOHN WESLEY.	HISTORY OF THE FREE-
THE YOUNG MAN IN THE	TRADE MOVEMENT IN
BATTLE OF LIFE.	ENGLAND.

Poultry Keeper, The Practical. By L. WRIGHT. With Coloured Plates and Illustrations. 3s. 6d.

Poultry, The Illustrated Book of. By L. WRIGHT. With Fifty Exquisite Coloured Plates, and numerous Wood Engravings. Cloth, 31s. 6d. ; half-morocco, £2 2s.

Poultry, The Book of. By LEWIS WRIGHT. *Popular Edition.* With Illustrations on Wood, 10s. 6d.

Quiver Yearly Volume, The. With about 300 Original Contributions by Eminent Divines and Popular Authors, and upwards of 250 high-class Illustrations. 7s. 6d.

Rabbit-Keeper, The Practical. By CUNICULUS. Illustrated. 3s. 6d.

Rays from the Realms of Nature. By the Rev. J. NEIL, M.A. Illustrated. 2s. 6d.

Red Library of English and American Classics, The. Stiff covers, 1s. each; cloth, 2s. each; or half-calf, marbled edges, 5s.

WASHINGTON IRVING'S SKETCH BOOK.	AMERICAN HUMOUR.
THE LAST DAYS of PALMYRA.	SKETCHES BY BOZ.
TALES OF THE BORDERS.	MACAULAY'S LAYS, AND SELECTED ESSAYS.
PRIDE AND PREJUDICE.	HARRY LORREQUER.
THE LAST of the MOHICANS.	THE OLD CURIOSITY SHOP.
THE HEART of MIDLOTHIAN.	RIENZI.
THE LAST DAYS of POMPEII.	THE TALISMAN.

Romeo and Juliet. *Édition de Luxe.* Illustrated with Twelve Superb Photogravures from Original Drawings by F. DICKSEE, A.R.A. £5 5s.

Royal River, The: The Thames from Source to Sea. With Descriptive Text and a Series of beautiful Engravings. £2 2s.

Russia. By D. MACKENZIE WALLACE, M.A. 5s.

Russo-Turkish War, Cassell's History of. With about 500 Illustrations. Two Vols., 9s. each.

Sandwith, Humphry. A Memoir by his Nephew, THOMAS HUMPHRY WARD. 7s. 6d.

Saturday Journal, Cassell's. Yearly Volume. 6s.

Science for All. Edited by Dr. ROBERT BROWN, M.A., F.L.S., &c. With 1,500 Illustrations. Five Vols. 9s. each.

Sea, The: Its Stirring Story of Adventure, Peril, and Heroism. By F. WHYMPER. With 400 Illustrations. Four Vols., 7s. 6d. each.

Shakspere, The Leopold. With 400 Illustrations. Cloth, 6s.

Shakspere, The Royal. With Steel Plates and Wood Engravings. Three Vols. 15s. each.

Shakespeare, Cassell's Quarto Edition. Edited by CHARLES and MARY COWDEN CLARKE, and containing about 600 Illustrations by H. C. SELOUS. Complete in Three Vols., cloth gilt, £3 3s.

Sketching from Nature in Water Colours. By AARON PENLEY. With Illustrations in Chromo-Lithography. 15s.

Smith, The Adventures and Discourses of Captain John. By JOHN ASHTON. Illustrated. 5s.

Sports and Pastimes, Cassell's Book of. With more than 800 Illustrations and Coloured Frontispiece. 768 pages. 7s. 6d.

Steam Engine, The Theory and Action of the: for Practical Men. By W. H. NORTHCOTT, C.E. 3s. 6d.

Stock Exchange Year-Book, The. By THOMAS SKINNER. 10s. 6d.

Stones of London, The. By E. F. FLOWER. 6d.

"Stories from Cassell's." 6d. each; cloth lettered, 9d. each.

MY AUNT'S MATCH-MAKING.	"RUNNING PILOT."
TOLD BY HER SISTER.	THE MORTGAGE MONEY.
THE SILVER LOCK.	GOURLAY BROTHERS.

A GREAT MISTAKE.

₊ The above are also issued, Three Volumes in One, cloth, price 2s. each.

Sunlight and Shade. With numerous Exquisite Engravings. 7s. 6d.

Telegraph Guide, The. Illustrated. 1s.

Trajan. An American Novel. By H. F. KEENAN. 7s. 6d.

Transformations of Insects, The. By Prof. P. MARTIN DUNCAN, M.B., F.R.S. With 240 Illustrations. 6s.

Treatment, The Year-Book of. A Critical Review for Practitioners of Medicine and Surgery. 5s.

United States, Cassell's History of the. By EDMUND OLLIER. With 600 Illustrations. Three Vols. 9s. each.

United States, Constitutional History and Political Development of the. By SIMON STERNE, of the New York Bar. 5s.

Universal History, Cassell's Illustrated. Four Vols. 9s. each.

Vicar of Wakefield and other Works by OLIVER GOLDSMITH. Illustrated. 3s. 6d.

Wealth Creation. By A. MONGREDIEN. 5s.

Westall, W., Novels by. *Popular Editions.* Cloth, 2s. each.

RALPH NORDRECK'S TRUST.
THE OLD FACTORY.   RED RYVINGTON.

What Girls Can Do. By PHYLLIS BROWNE. 2s. 6d.

Wild Animals and Birds: their Haunts and Habits. By Dr. ANDREW WILSON. Illustrated. 7s. 6d.

Wild Birds, Familiar. First and Second Series. By W. SWAYSLAND. With 40 Coloured Plates in each. 12s. 6d. each.

Wild Flowers, Familiar. By F. E. HULME, F.L.S., F.S.A. Five Series. With 40 Coloured Plates in each. 12s. 6d. each.

Winter in India, A. By the Rt. Hon. W. E. BAXTER, M.P. 5s.

Wise Woman, The. By GEORGE MACDONALD. 2s. 6d.

Wood Magic: A Fable. By RICHARD JEFFERIES. 6s.

World of the Sea. Translated from the French of MOQUIN TANDON, by the Very Rev. H. MARTYN HART, M.A. Illustrated. Cloth. 6s.

World of Wit and Humour, The. With 400 Illustrations. Cloth, 7s. 6d.; cloth gilt, gilt edges, 10s. 6d.

World of Wonders. Two Vols. With 400 Illustrations. 7s. 6d. each.

MAGAZINES.

The Quiver, for Sunday Reading. Monthly, 6d.

Cassell's Family Magazine. Monthly, 7d.

"Little Folks" Magazine. Monthly, 6d.

The Magazine of Art. Monthly, 1s.

Cassell's Saturday Journal. Weekly, 1d.; Monthly, 6d.

. *Full particulars of CASSELL & COMPANY'S Monthly Serial Publications, numbering upwards of 50 different Works, will be found in CASSELL & COMPANY'S COMPLETE CATALOGUE, sent post free on application.*

Catalogues of CASSELL & COMPANY'S PUBLICATIONS, which may be had at all Booksellers', or will be sent post free on application to the publishers:—

CASSELL'S COMPLETE CATALOGUE, containing particulars of One Thousand Volumes.

CASSELL'S CLASSIFIED CATALOGUE, in which their Works are arranged according to price, from *Sixpence to Twenty-five Guineas.*

CASSELL'S EDUCATIONAL CATALOGUE, containing particulars of CASSELL & COMPANY'S Educational Works and Students' Manuals.

CASSELL & COMPANY, LIMITED, *Ludgate Hill, London.*

Bibles and Religious Works.

Bible, The Crown Illustrated. With about 1,000 Original Illustrations. With References, &c. 1,248 pages, crown 4to, cloth, 7s. 6d.

Bible, Cassell's Illustrated Family. With 900 Illustrations. Leather, gilt edges, £2 10s.

Bible Dictionary. Cassell's. With nearly 600 Illustrations. 7s. 6d.

Bible Educator, The. Edited by the Very Rev. Dean PLUMPTRE, D.D., Wells. With Illustrations, Maps, &c. Four Vols.; cloth, 6s. each.

Bunyan's Pilgrim's Progress (Cassell's Illustrated). Demy 4to. Illustrated throughout. 7s. 6d.

Bunyan's Pilgrim's Progress. With Illustrations. Cloth, 3s. 6d.

Bunyan's Holy War. With 100 Illustrations. Cloth, 7s. 6d.

Child's Life of Christ, The. Complete in One Handsome Volume, with about 200 Original Illustrations. Demy 4to, gilt edges, 21s.

Child's Bible, The. With 200 Illustrations. Demy 4to, 830 pp. 143rd *Thousand. Cheap Edition,* 7s. 6d.

Church at Home, The. A Series of Short Sermons. By the Rt. Rev. ROWLEY HILL, D.D., Bishop of Sodor and Man. 5s.

Day-Dawn in Dark Places; or Wanderings and Work in Bech-wanaland, South Africa. By the Rev. JOHN MACKENZIE. Illustrated throughout. Cloth, 3s. 6d.

Difficulties of Belief, Some. By the Rev. T. TEIGNMOUTH SHORE, M.A. *New and Cheap Edition.* 2s. 6d.

Doré Bible. With 230 Illustrations by GUSTAVE DORÉ. Cloth, £2 10s.; Persian morocco, £3 10s.

Early Days of Christianity, The. By the Ven. Archdeacon FARRAR, D.D.. F.R.S.
LIBRARY EDITION. Two Vols., 24s.; morocco, £2 2s.
POPULAR EDITION. Complete in One Volume, cloth, 6s.; cloth, gilt edges, 7s. 6d.; Persian morocco, 10s. 6d.; tree-calf, 15s.

Family Prayer-Book, The. Edited by Rev. Canon GARBETT. M.A., and Rev. S. MARTIN. Extra crown 4to, cloth, 5s.; morocco, 18s.

Geikie, Cunningham, .D.D., Works by:—
HOURS WITH THE BIBLE. Six Vols., 6s. each.
ENTERING ON LIFE. 3s. 6d.
THE PRECIOUS PROMISES. 2s. 6d.
THE ENGLISH REFORMATION. 5s.
OLD TESTAMENT CHARACTERS. 6s.
THE LIFE AND WORDS OF CHRIST. Two Vols., cloth, 30s. *Students' Edition.* Two Vols., 16s.

Glories of the Man of Sorrows, The. Sermons preached at St. James's, Piccadilly. By the Rev. H. G. BONAVIA HUNT. 2s. 6d.

Gospel of Grace, The. By A. LINDESIE. Cloth, 3s. 6d.

" Heart Chords." A Series of Works by Eminent Divines. Bound in cloth, red edges, One Shilling each.

MY FATHER.	MY SOUL.
MY BIBLE.	MY GROWTH IN DIVINE LIFE.
MY WORK FOR GOD.	MY HEREAFTER.
MY OBJECT IN LIFE.	MY WALK WITH GOD.
MY ASPIRATIONS.	MY AIDS TO THE DIVINE LIFE.
MY EMOTIONAL LIFE.	MY SOURCES OF STRENGTH.
MY BODY.	

Life of Christ, The. By the Ven. Archdeacon FARRAR, D.D., F.R.S., Chaplain-in-Ordinary to the Queen.

ILLUSTRATED EDITION, with about 300 Original Illustrations. Extra crown 4to, cloth, gilt edges, 21s.; morocco antique, 42s.

LIBRARY EDITION. Two Vols. Cloth, 24s.; morocco, 42s.

BIJOU EDITION. Five Volumes, in box, 10s. 6d. the set.

POPULAR EDITION, in One Vol. 8vo, cloth, 6s.; cloth, gilt edges, 7s. 6d.; Persian morocco, gilt edges, 10s. 6d.; tree-calf, 15s.

Marriage Ring, The. By WILLIAM LANDELS, D.D. Bound in white leatherette, gilt edges, in box, 6s.; morocco, 8s. 6d.

Martyrs, Foxe's Book of. With about 200 Illustrations. Imperial 8vo, 732 pages, cloth, 12s.; cloth gilt, gilt edges, 15s.

Moses and Geology; or, The Harmony of the Bible with Science. By SAMUEL KINNS, Ph.D., F.R.A.S. Illustrated. *Cheap Edition*, 6s.

Music of the Bible, The. By J. STAINER, M.A., Mus. Doc. 2s. 6d.

Near and the Heavenly Horizons, The. By the Countess DE GASPARIN. 1s.; cloth, 2s.

New Testament Commentary for English Readers, The. Edited by the Rt. Rev. C. J. ELLICOTT, D.D., Lord Bishop of Gloucester and Bristol. In Three Volumes, 21s. each.

Vol. I.—The Four Gospels.

Vol. II.—The Acts, Romans, Corinthians, Galatians.

Vol. III.—The remaining Books of the New Testament.

Old Testament Commentary for English Readers, The. Edited by the Right Rev. C. J. ELLICOTT, D.D., Lord Bishop of Gloucester and Bristol. Complete in 5 Vols., 21s. each.

Vol. I.—Genesis to Numbers.
Vol. II.—Deuteronomy to Samuel II.
Vol. III.—Kings I. to Esther.
Vol. IV.—Job to Isaiah.
Vol. V.—Jeremiah to Malachi.

Patriarchs, The. By the late Rev. W. HANNA, D.D., and the Ven. Archdeacon NORRIS, B.D. 2s. 6d.

Protestantism, The History of. By the Rev. J. A. WYLIE, LL.D. Containing upwards of 600 Original Illustrations. Three Vols., 27s.

Quiver Yearly Volume, The. 350 high-class Illustrations. 7s. 6d.

Revised Version—Commentary on the Revised Version of the New Testament. By the Rev. W. G. HUMPHRY, B.D. 7s. 6d.

Sacred Poems, The Book of. Edited by the Rev. Canon BAYNES, M.A. With Illustrations. Cloth, gilt edges, 5s.

St. George for England; and other Sermons preached to Children. By the Rev. T. TEIGNMOUTH SHORE, M.A. 5s.

St. Paul, The Life and Work of. By the Ven. Archdeacon FARRAR, D.D., F.R.S., Chaplain in Ordinary to the Queen.

LIBRARY EDITION. Two Vols., cloth, 24s.; morocco, 42s.

ILLUSTRATED EDITION, complete in One Volume, with about 300 Illustrations, £1 1s.; morocco, £2 2s.

POPULAR EDITION. One Volume, 8vo, cloth, 6s.; cloth, gilt edges, 7s. 6d.; Persian morocco, 10s. 6d.; tree-calf, 15s.

Secular Life, The Gospel of the. Sermons preached at Oxford. By the Hon. W. H. FREMANTLE, Canon of Canterbury. 5s.

Sermons Preached at Westminster Abbey. By ALFRED BARRY, D.D., D.C.L., Primate of Australia. 5s.

Shall We Know One Another? By the Rt. Rev. J. C. RYLE, D.D., Bishop of Liverpool. *New and Enlarged Edition.* Cloth limp, 1s.

Simon Peter: His Life, Times, and Friends. By E. HODDER. 5s.

Voice of Time, The. By JOHN STROUD. Cloth gilt, 1s.

Educational Works and Students' Manuals.

Algebra, The Elements of. By Prof. WALLACE, M.A., 1s.

Arithmetics, The Modern School. By GEORGE RICKS, B.Sc. Lond. With Test Cards. *(List on application.)*

Book-Keeping:—
Book-Keeping for Schools. By Theodore Jones, 2s.; cloth, 3s.
Book-Keeping for the Million. By T. Jones, 2s.; cloth, 3s.
Books for Jones's System. Ruled Sets of, 2s.

Commentary, The New Testament. Edited by the Lord Bishop of GLOUCESTER and BRISTOL. Handy Volume Edition. St. Matthew, 3s. 6d. St. Mark, 3s. St. Luke, 3s. 6d. St. John, 3s. 6d. The Acts of the Apostles, 3s. 6d. Romans, 2s. 6d. Corinthians I. and II., 3s. Galatians, Ephesians, and Philippians, 3s. Colossians, Thessalonians, and Timothy, 3s. Titus, Philemon, Hebrews, and James, 3s. Peter, Jude, and John, 3s. The Revelation, 3s. An Introduction to the New Testament, 3s. 6d.

Commentary, Old Testament. Edited by Bishop ELLICOTT. Handy Volume Edition. In Vols. suitable for School and general use. Genesis, 3s. 6d. Exodus, 3s. Leviticus, 3s. Numbers, 2s. 6d. Deuteronomy, 2s. 6d.

Copy-Books, Cassell's Graduated. *Eighteen Books.* 2d. each.

Copy-Books, The Modern School. In Twelve Books, of 24 pages each, price 2d. each.

Drawing Books for Young Artists. 4 Books. 6d. each.

Drawing Books, Superior. 4 Books. Printed in Fac-simile by Lithography, price 5s. each.

Drawing Copies, Cassell's Modern School Freehand. First Grade, 1s.; Second Grade, 2s.

Energy and Motion: A Text-Book of Elementary Mechanics. By WILLIAM PAICE, M.A. Illustrated. 1s. 6d.

English Literature, A First Sketch of, from the Earliest Period to the Present Time. By Prof. HENRY MORLEY. 7s. 6d.

Euclid, Cassell's. Edited by Prof. WALLACE, A.M. 1s.

Euclid, The First Four Books of. In paper, 6d.; cloth, 9d.

French, Cassell's Lessons in. *New and Revised Edition.* Parts I. and II., each 2s. 6d.; complete, 4s. 6d. Key, 1s. 6d.

French-English and English-French Dictionary. *Entirely New and Enlarged Edition.* 1,150 pages, 8vo, cloth, 3s. 6d.

Galbraith and Haughton's Scientific Manuals. By the Rev. Prof. GALBRAITH, M.A., and the Rev. Prof. HAUGHTON, M.D., D.C.L. Arithmetic, 3s. 6d.—Plane Trigonometry, 2s. 6d.—Euclid, Books I., II., III., 2s. 6d.—Books IV., V., VI. 2s. 6d.—Mathematical Tables, 3s. 6d.—Mechanics, 3s. 6d.—Optics, 2s. 6d.—Hydrostatics, 3s. 6d.—Astronomy, 5s.—Steam Engine, 3s. 6d.—Algebra, Part I., cloth, 2s. 6d.; Complete, 7s. 6d.—Tides and Tidal Currents, with Tidal Cards, 3s.

German-English and English-German Dictionary. 3s. 6d.

German Reading, First Lessons in. By A. JAGST. Illustrated. 1s.

Handbook of New Code of Regulations. By JOHN F. Moss. 1s.

Historical Course for Schools, Cassell's. Illustrated throughout. I.—Stories from English History, 1s. II.—The Simple Outline of English History, 1s. 3d. III.—The Class History of England, 2s. 6d.

Latin-English and English-Latin Dictionary. By J. R. BEARD, D.D., and C. BEARD, B.A. Crown 8vo, 914 pp., 3s. 6d.

Little Folks' History of England. By ISA CRAIG-KNOX. With 30 Illustrations. 1s. 6d.

Making of the Home, The: A Book of Domestic Economy for School and Home Use. By Mrs. SAMUEL A. BARNETT. 1s. 6d.

Marlborough Books:—Arithmetic Examples, 3s. Arithmetic Rules, 1s. 6d. French Exercises, 3s. 6d. French Grammar, 2s. 6d. German Grammar, 3s. 6d.

Music, An Elementary Manual of. By HENRY LESLIE. 1s.

Natural Philosophy. By Rev. Prof. HAUGHTON, F.R.S. Illustrated. 3s. 6d.

Painting, Guides to. With Coloured Plates and full instructions:—Animal Painting, 5s.—China Painting, 5s.—Figure Painting, 7s. 6d.—Flower Painting, 2 Books, 5s. each.—Tree Painting, 5s.—Sepia Painting, 5s.—Water Colour Painting, 5s.—Neutral Tint, 5s.

Popular Educator, Cassell's. *New and Thoroughly Revised Edition.* Illustrated throughout. Complete in Six Vols., 5s. each.

Physical Science, Intermediate Text-Book of. By F. H. BOWMAN, D.Sc. F.R.A.S., F.L.S. Illustrated. 3s. 6d.

Readers, Cassell's Readable. Carefully graduated, extremely interesting, and illustrated throughout. (*List on application.*)

Readers, Cassell's Historical. Illustrated throughout, printed on superior paper, and strongly bound in cloth. (*List on application.*)

Readers, The Modern Geographical, illustrated throughout, and strongly bound in cloth. (*List on application.*)

Readers, The Modern School. Illustrated. (*List on application.*)

Reading and Spelling Book, Cassell's Illustrated. 1s.

Right Lines; or, Form and Colour. With Illustrations. 1s.

School Manager's Manual. By F. C. MILLS, M.A. 1s.

Shakspere's Plays for School Use. 5 Books. Illustrated, 6d. each.

Shakspere Reading Book, The. By H. COURTHOPE BOWEN, M.A. Illustrated. 3s. 6d. Also issued in Three Books, 1s. each.

Spelling, A Complete Manual of. By J. D. MORELL, LL.D. 1s.

Technical Manuals, Cassell's. Illustrated throughout:—Handrailing and Staircasing, 3s. 6d.—Bricklayers, Drawing for, 3s.—Building Construction, 2s.—Cabinet-Makers, Drawing for, 3s.—Carpenters and Joiners, Drawing for, 3s. 6d.—Gothic Stonework, 3s.—Linear Drawing and Practical Geometry, 2s.—Linear Drawing and Projection, The Two Vols. in One, 3s. 6d.—Machinists and Engineers, Drawing for, 4s. 6d.—Metal-Plate Workers, Drawing for, 3s.—Model Drawing, 3s.—Orthographical and Isometrical Projection, 2s.—Practical Perspective, 3s.—Stonemasons, Drawing for, 3s.—Applied Mechanics, by Prof. R. S. Ball, LL.D., 2s.—Systematic Drawing and Shading, by Charles Ryan, 2s.

Technical Educator, Cassell's. Four Vols., 6s. each. Popular Edition, in Four Vols., 5s. each.

Technology, Manuals of. Edited by Prof. AYRTON, F.R.S., and RICHARD WORMELL, D.Sc., M.A. Illustrated throughout:—The Dyeing of Textile Fabrics, by Prof. Hummel, 5s.—Watch and Clock Making, by D. Glasgow, 4s. 6d.—Steel and Iron, by W. H. Greenwood, F.C.S., Assoc. M.I.C.E., &c., 5s.—Spinning Woollen and Worsted, by W. S. Bright McLaren, 4s. 6d.—Design in Textile Fabrics, by T. R. Ashenhurst, 4s. 6d.—Practical Mechanics, by Prof. Perry, M.E., 3s. 6d.—Cutting Tools Worked by Hand and Machine, by Prof. Smith, 3s. 6d.

Other Volumes in preparation. A Prospectus sent post free on application.

Books for Young People.

"**Little Folks**" Half-Yearly Volume. With 200 Illustrations, 3s. 6d.; or cloth gilt, 5s.

Bo-Peep. A Book for the Little Ones. With Original Stories and Verses, Illustrated throughout. Boards, 2s. 6d.; cloth gilt, 3s. 6d.

The World's Lumber Room. By SELINA GAYE. Illustrated. 3s. 6d.

The "Proverbs" Series. Consisting of a New and Original Series of Stories by Popular Authors, founded on and illustrating well-known Proverbs. With Four Illustrations in each Book, printed on a tint. Crown 8vo, 160 pages, cloth, 1s. each.

FRITTERS; OR, "IT'S A LONG LANE THAT HAS NO TURNING." By Sarah Pitt.

TRIXY; OR, "THOSE WHO LIVE IN GLASS HOUSES SHOULDN'T THROW STONES." By Maggie Symington.

THE TWO HARDCASTLES; OR, "A FRIEND IN NEED IS A FRIEND INDEED." By Madeline Bonavia Hunt.

MAJOR MONK'S MOTTO; OR, "LOOK BEFORE YOU LEAP." By the Rev. F. Langbridge.

TIM THOMSON'S TRIAL; OR, "ALL IS NOT GOLD THAT GLITTERS." By George Weatherly.

URSULA'S STUMBLING-BLOCK; OR, "PRIDE COMES BEFORE A FALL." By Julia Goddard.

RUTH'S LIFE-WORK; OR, "NO PAINS, NO GAINS." By the Rev. Joseph Johnson.

The "Cross and Crown" Series. Consisting of Stories founded on incidents which occurred during Religious Persecutions of Past Days. With Four Illustrations in each Book, printed on a tint. Crown 8vo, 256 pages, 2s. 6d. each.

BY FIRE AND SWORD: A STORY OF THE HUGUENOTS. By Thomas Archer.

ADAM HEPBURN'S VOW: A TALE OF KIRK AND COVENANT. By Annie S. Swan.

No. XIII.; OR, THE STORY OF THE LOST VESTAL. A Tale of Early Christian Days. By Emma Marshall.

The World's Workers. A Series of New and Original Volumes. With Portraits printed on a tint as Frontispiece. 1s. each.

CHARLES DICKENS. By his Eldest Daughter.

SIR TITUS SALT AND GEORGE MOORE. By J. Burnley.

FLORENCE NIGHTINGALE, CATHERINE MARSH, FRANCES RIDLEY HAVERGAL, MRS. RANVARD ("L.N.R."). By Lizzie Aldridge.

DR. GUTHRIE, FATHER MATHEW, ELIHU BURRITT, GEORGE LIVESEY. By the Rev. J. W. Kirton.

SIR HENRY HAVELOCK AND COLIN CAMPBELL, LORD CLYDE. By E. C. Phillips.

ABRAHAM LINCOLN. By Ernest Foster.

DAVID LIVINGSTONE. · By Robert Smiles.

GEORGE MÜLLER AND ANDREW REED. By E. R. Pitman.

RICHARD COBDEN. By R. Gowing.

BENJAMIN FRANKLIN. By E. M. Tomkinson.

HANDEL. By Eliza Clarke.

TURNER, THE ARTIST. By the Rev. S. A. Swaine.

GEORGE AND ROBERT STEPHENSON. By C. L. Matéaux.

The "Chimes" Series. Each containing 64 pages, with Illustrations on every page, and handsomely bound in cloth, 1s.

BIBLE CHIMES. Contains Bible Verses for Every Day in the Month.

DAILY CHIMES. Verses from the Poets for Every Day in the Month.

HOLY CHIMES. Verses for Every Sunday in the Year.

OLD WORLD CHIMES. Verses from old writers for Every Day in the Month.

New Books for Boys. With Original Illustrations, produced in a tint. Cloth gilt, 5s. each.

"FOLLOW MY LEADER;" OR, THE BOYS OF TEMPLETON. By Talbot Baines Reed.

FOR FORTUNE AND GLORY: A STORY OF THE SOUDAN WAR. By Lewis Hough.

THE CHAMPION OF ODIN; OR, VIKING LIFE IN THE DAYS OF OLD. By J. Fred. Hodgetts.

BOUND BY A SPELL; OR THE HUNTED WITCH OF THE FOREST. By the Hon. Mrs. Greene.

Price 3s. 6d. each.

ON BOARD THE "ESMERALDA;" OR, MARTIN LEIGH'S LOG. By John C. Hutcheson.

IN QUEST OF GOLD; OR, UNDER THE WHANGA FALLS. By Alfred St. Johnston.

FOR QUEEN AND KING; OR, THE LOYAL 'PRENTICE. By Henry Frith.

The "Boy Pioneer" Series. By EDWARD S. ELLIS. With Four Full-page Illustrations in each Book. Crown 8vo, cloth, 2s. 6d. each.

NED IN THE WOODS. A Tale of Early Days in the West.

NED ON THE RIVER. A Tale of Indian River Warfare.

NED IN THE BLOCK HOUSE. A Story of Pioneer Life in Kentucky.

The "Log Cabin" Series. By EDWARD S. ELLIS. With Four Full-page Illustrations in each. Crown 8vo, cloth, 2s. 6d. each.

THE LOST TRAIL. | CAMP-FIRE AND WIGWAM.

Sixpenny Story Books. All Illustrated, and containing Interesting Stories by well-known Writers.

LITTLE CONTENT.
THE SMUGGLER'S CAVE.
LITTLE LIZZIE.
LITTLE BIRD.
THE BOOT ON THE WRONG FOOT.
LUKE BARNICOTT.
LITTLE PICKLES.
THE BOAT CLUB. By Oliver Optic.

HELPFUL NELLIE; AND OTHER STORIES.
THE ELCHESTER COLLEGE BOYS.
MY FIRST CRUISE.
LOTTIE'S WHITE FROCK.
ONLY JUST ONCE.
THE LITTLE PEACEMAKER.
THE DELFT JUG. By Silverpen.

The "Baby's Album" Series. Four Books, each containing about 50 Illustrations. Price 6d. each; or cloth gilt, 1s. each.

BABY'S ALBUM.
DOLLY'S ALBUM.

FAIRY'S ALBUM.
PUSSY'S ALBUM.

Illustrated Books for the Little Ones. Containing interesting Stories. All Illustrated. 1s. each.

INDOORS AND OUT.
SOME FARM FRIENDS.
THOSE GOLDEN SANDS.
LITTLE MOTHERS AND THEIR CHILDREN.

OUR PRETTY PETS.
OUR SCHOOLDAY HOURS.
CREATURES TAME.
CREATURES WILD.

Shilling Story Books. All Illustrated, and containing Interesting Stories.

THORNS AND TANGLES.
THE CUCKOO IN THE ROBIN'S NEST.
JOHN'S MISTAKE.
PEARL'S FAIRY FLOWER.
THE HISTORY OF FIVE LITTLE PITCHERS.
DIAMONDS IN THE SAND.
SURLY BOB.
THE GIANT'S CRADLE.

SHAG AND DOLL.
AUNT LUCIA'S LOCKET.
THE MAGIC MIRROR.
THE COST OF REVENGE.
CLEVER FRANK.
AMONG THE REDSKINS.
THE FERRYMAN OF BRILL.
HARRY MAXWELL.
A BANISHED MONARCH.

" Little Folks " Painting Books. With Text, and Outline Illustrations for Water-Colour Painting. 1s. each.

FRUITS AND BLOSSOMS FOR "LITTLE FOLKS" TO PAINT.
THE "LITTLE FOLKS", PROVERB PAINTING BOOK.
THE "LITTLE FOLKS" ILLUMINATING BOOK.

PICTURES TO PAINT.
"LITTLE FOLKS" PAINTING BOOK.
"LITTLE FOLKS" NATURE PAINTING BOOK.
ANOTHER "LITTLE FOLKS" PAINTING BOOK.

Eighteenpenny Story Books. All Illustrated throughout.

THREE WEE ULSTER LASSIES.
LITTLE QUEEN MAB.
UP THE LADDER.
DICK'S HERO ; AND OTHER STORIES.
THE CHIP BOY.
RAGGLES, BAGGLES, and the EMPEROR.
ROSES FROM THORNS.
FAITH'S FATHER.

BY LAND AND SEA.
THE YOUNG BERRINGTONS.
JEFF AND LEFF.
TOM MORRIS'S ERROR.
WORTH MORE THAN GOLD.
" THROUGH FLOOD — THROUGH FIRE ;" AND OTHER STORIES.
THE GIRL WITH THE GOLDEN LOCKS.
STORIES OF THE OLDEN TIME.

The " Cosy Corner " Series. Story Books for Children. Each containing nearly ONE HUNDRED PICTURES. 1s. 6d. each.

SEE-SAW STORIES.
LITTLE CHIMES FOR ALL TIMES.
WEE WILLIE WINKIE.
BRIGHT SUNDAYS.
PET'S POSY OF PICTURES AND STORIES.
DOT'S STORY BOOK.

STORY FLOWERS for RAINY HOURS.
LITTLE TALKS with LITTLE PEOPLE
BRIGHT RAYS FOR DULL DAYS.
CHATS FOR SMALL CHATTERERS.
PICTURES FOR HAPPY HOURS.
UPS AND DOWNS OF A DONKEY'S LIFE.

The " World in Pictures." Illustrated throughout. 2s. 6d. each.

A RAMBLE ROUND FRANCE.
ALL THE RUSSIAS.
CHATS ABOUT GERMANY.
THE LAND OF THE PYRAMIDS (EGYPT).
PEEPS INTO CHINA.

THE EASTERN WONDERLAND (JAPAN).
GLIMPSES OF SOUTH AMERICA.
ROUND AFRICA.
THE LAND OF TEMPLES (INDIA).
THE ISLES OF THE PACIFIC.

Two-Shilling Story Books. All Illustrated.

STORIES OF THE TOWER.
MR. BURKE'S NIECES.
MAY CUNNINGHAM'S TRIAL.
THE TOP OF THE LADDER : HOW TO REACH IT.
LITTLE FLOTSAM.
MADGE AND HER FRIENDS.
THE CHILDREN OF THE COURT.
A MOONBEAM TANGLE.
MAID MARJORY.

THE FOUR CATS OF THE TIPPERTONS.
MARION'S TWO HOMES.
LITTLE FOLKS' SUNDAY BOOK.
TWO FOURPENNY BITS.
POOR NELLY.
TOM HERIOT.
THROUGH PERIL TO FORTUNE.
AUNT TABITHA'S WAIFS.
IN MISCHIEF AGAIN.

Half-Crown Story Books.

MARGARET'S ENEMY.
PEN'S PERPLEXITIES.
NOTABLE SHIPWRECKS.
GOLDEN DAYS.
WONDERS OF COMMON THINGS.
LITTLE EMPRESS JOAN.
TRUTH WILL OUT.

SOLDIER AND PATRIOT (George Washington).
PICTURES OF SCHOOL LIFE AND BOYHOOD.
THE YOUNG MAN IN THE BATTLE OF LIFE. By the Rev Dr. Landels.
THE TRUE GLORY OF WOMAN. By the Rev. Dr. Landels.

www.ingramcontent.com/pod-product-compliance
Lightning Source LLC
Chambersburg PA
CBHW031122020726
47495CB00007B/2304